Contents

Introduction ....

Chapter 1 – Overview and Signing Up 7

    Wix Subscription Plans 7

    Signing Up For an Account 9

    Selecting Your Website Type (Templates and ADI) 13

Chapter 2 - The Wix Interface 17

    Wix Editor 17

    Text Based Menus 19

    Wix Toolbar 22

    Main Navigation Buttons 25

    Strips 27

    Rulers 29

    Gridlines 31

    Media Manager 33

Chapter 3 – Creating a New Website 40

    Creating a New Blank Website 41

    Choosing a New Template 44

    Website Preview 46

Chapter 4 – Adding Design Elements 49

    The Add Button 49

    Strips 51

    Backgrounds 55

Headers and Footers 59

Adding Text 61

Adding Images 66

Buttons 74

Videos 78

Object Animations 88

Right Click Options 90

Chapter 5 – Adding Pages 92

Adding and Managing Your Pages 92

Subpages 97

Page Transitions 98

Page Settings 99

Navigation Menu Management 100

Chapter 6 – Advanced Features 106

Creating Links and Anchors 106

Anchors 110

Site Favicon 115

Slider Image Gallery 116

Social Tools 120

Embedding Objects 123

Contact Forms 130

Location Maps 135

Blogs 139

Wix Logo Maker Website 144

SEO (Search Engine Optimization) 150

Site Search Box 160

WIX
MADE EASY

Professional Websites Created With Ease

By James Bernstein

Installing Apps 162

Chapter 7 - Tools and Settings 168

Wix Dashboard 169

Content Manager 175

Roles and Permissions 186

Transferring Site Ownership 190

Restore Previous Versions (Site History) 192

Using the Search Bar to Find Wix Elements 196

Make a Duplicate Copy of Your Website 198

Mobile Editor\Viewer 200

Chapter 8 - Publishing Your Website 209

Publishing and Unpublishing Your Website 209

Change Your Website URL 211

Connect Your Domain or Get Your Own From Wix 212

Wix Free SSL Certificate 214

Getting a Custom Email Address 215

What's Next? 217

About the Author 219

Introduction

Since the internet has been around since 1983 (depending on who you ask), you would think that there are many websites available for you to visit and you would most definitely be right. Websites come and go with new sites popping up daily and if you are a business owner and don't have your own website then you are not running your business up to its full potential.

Nowadays, the internet is the first place people go when they are looking to buy a new product or get some type of service. In fact, the internet is where most people go when looking for just about anything. So if you have something you want to share with the world, creating a website for it is the best way to get your products, services or ideas out there.

Wix is one of the most popular and easy to use website creation tools, and you don't need any HTML (HyperText Markup Language) coding experience to use it and is fairly easy to get a basic website up and running in a short amount of time. And if you want to put a little extra effort into your work, you can create a very professional site for your business or personal use. And best of all, it's free to use and publish your site on the internet for all to see!

If you have used software such as Google Slides, Google Sites, Microsoft PowerPoint or Microsoft Publisher then you should have no problem getting up and running with Wix since it uses some of the same processes as these other programs where you simply drag and drop text and images where you would like them to go. Of course, there is a little more to it than that but after you spend some time with Wix you should get the hang of it fairly quickly even though can look a little intimidating the first time you use it.

The goal of this book is to get you up and running with Wix and show you how to make great looking websites for your business or personal use. I will also go over many of the other advanced features such as how to publish your website online and even how to use your own custom domain name. Even though Wix is a fairly easy application to use, there are many, many things you can do with it so covering each and every feature would make this a 2000 page book! Once you get a hang of the basics and know where to find the tools you are looking for it should be easy to figure out anything that I might not have covered. So on that note, let's get our ideas online!

Chapter 1 – Overview and Signing Up

You might have noticed the trend these days with many applications being used online rather than installed on to your desktop computer. By having these apps run online or "in the cloud", it allows you to access your work from almost any device that has an internet connection from any location.

This also allows the app developers more control over how and when their applications are used and updated and also saves them from needing to develop software that needs to be installed on your computer. For example, if you have been using Microsoft Office for a period of time you might have noticed that they are moving from the desktop versions of their programs such as Word and Excel to online versions used in their Office 365 subscription version and Office for the Web free version.

If you are interested in learning how to use Microsoft's Office for the Web online productivity apps then check out my book titled **Office for the Web Made Easy.**
https://www.amazon.com/dp/B092H828GK

With that being said, you will be doing all of your design work within your web browser rather than using a program or application installed on your computer. This doesn't mean that you can't do things such as edit your photos or other design elements on your PC because you can do this type of thing and then upload them to your Wix account to be used on your site.

Wix Subscription Plans
When you first start using Wix I would recommend that you just stick with the basic\free plan to make sure that it is the platform that you want to use to create your website. Then if the design and site functionality end up working for your business or personal site then you can go with one of the pay for (premium) plans.

There are many paid subscriptions to choose from and there are also three categories, each with different plans. There are the *Website* Plans, *Business & eCommerce* Plans, and *Enterprise* Plans. For the sake of this section I will be discussing the Website Plans category since that is most likely where you will be going when it's time to choose a subscription.

Figure 1.1 shows the four plans that are in the Website Plans category and as you can see, each one offers more features as the price goes up. When you go to the Wix website for yourself, you might see different numbers for the pricing based on when Wix either raises their prices or offers discounted temporary deals.

	Website Plans Great for showcasing a professional site		Business & eCommerce Plans Essential for accepting online payments		Enterprise Plans Custom solutions tailored to your brand
		VIP First Priority Support $39 /month Select	Pro Complete Online Branding $23 /month Select	Unlimited Entrepreneurs & Freelancers $18 /month Select	Combo For Personal Use $14 /month Select
Custom Domain	ⓘ	✓	✓	✓	✓
Free Domain for 1 Year	ⓘ	✓	✓	✓	✓
Remove Wix Ads	ⓘ	✓	✓	✓	✓
Free SSL Certificate	ⓘ	✓	✓	✓	✓
Storage Space	ⓘ	35GB	20GB	10GB	3GB
Video Hours	ⓘ	5 Hours	2 Hours	1 Hour	30 Minutes
$300 Ad Vouchers	ⓘ	✓	✓	✓	
Site Booster App Free for 1 Year	ⓘ	✓	✓	✓	
Visitor Analytics App Free for 1 Year	ⓘ	✓	✓	✓	
Events Calendar App Free for 1 Year	ⓘ	✓	✓		
Professional Logo	ⓘ	✓	✓		
Social Media Logo Files	ⓘ	✓	✓		
Customer Care	ⓘ	Priority Customer Care	24/7 Customer Care	24/7 Customer Care	24/7 Customer Care

Figure 1.1

One of the main reasons to get a subscription plan is to remove the Wix ads that will be placed on your website once you publish it using the free account. If your site is just for something like your baseball team or school project this might be fine but if you are using it for your business then it might not look that professional.

You might also want to have your own custom domain, so your website address (URL) doesn't contain their name in it. The format of the free account address is **username.wixsite.com** and you might not want wixsite.com for your domain name and might want your own personalized one instead. Just keep in mind that whatever you choose for your domain name will need to be available and not in use by someone else.

Another thing to consider when deciding if you want to go with the free vs. paid plan is storage space for things such as images and videos. The free account only gets you 500MB of space where the paid accounts get you 3GB up to 35GB depending on which one you choose.

Signing Up For an Account
The first thing you will need to do before starting on your website is sign up for a Wix account using your email address. Then you will need to log in with this account whenever you wish to work on your website. All of your site data will be stored with Wix on their end so make sure you remember your login information!

To sign up for an account, simply go to the Wix website at **wix.com** and click on the *Get Started* button to create your account. Then you will enter your email address and create a secure password to be used for logging in.

The first time you login you might be presented with a screen that will ask you a few questions to try and get an idea of what type of website you are trying to create.

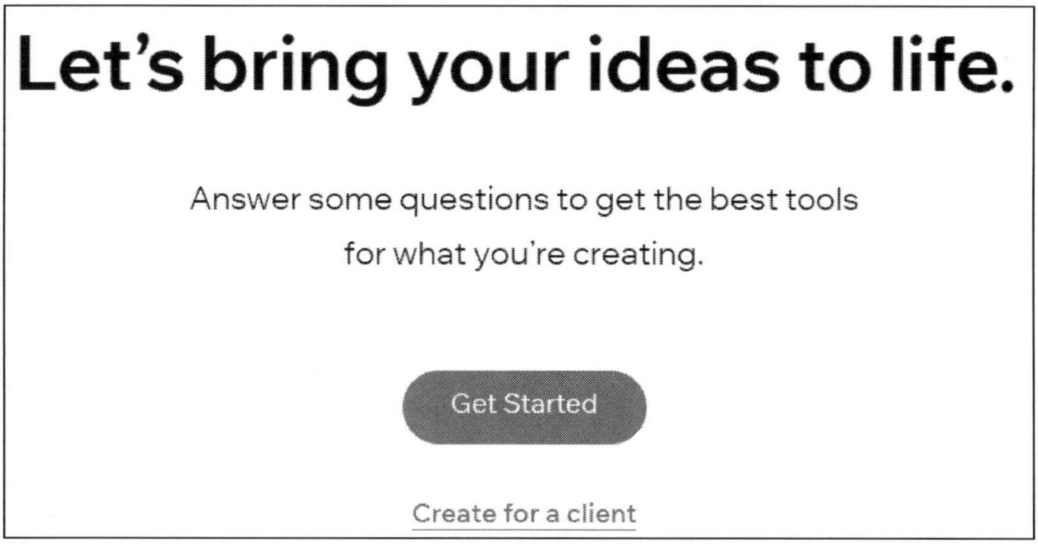

Let's bring your ideas to life.

Answer some questions to get the best tools

for what you're creating.

Get Started

Create for a client

Figure 1.2

Here you can enter your business type to have Wix look for templates or designs that match what you typed in to save you some time when it comes to creating your design.

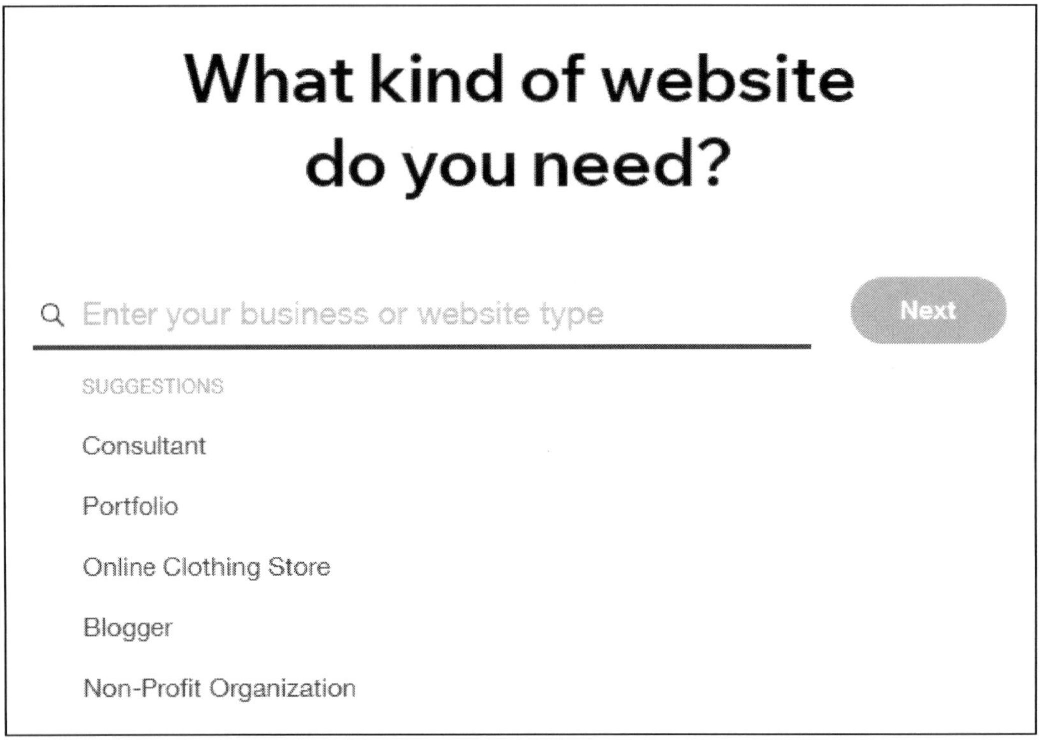

What kind of website do you need?

Q Enter your business or website type   Next

SUGGESTIONS

Consultant

Portfolio

Online Clothing Store

Blogger

Non-Profit Organization

Figure 1.3

I will be creating a site for the **Triple C Bakery** (Cupcakes, Cookies and Cakes) so I will enter *bakery* for the type of business I have. As you can see in figure 1.4, it gives some additional suggestions related to the word bakery.

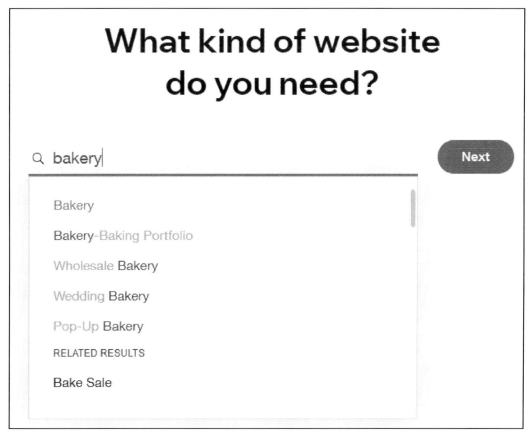

Figure 1.4

Now that Wix knows what type of website I will be creating, it will offer suggestions as to what types of features I can add to my site, and I can check the box next to each one I want to add.

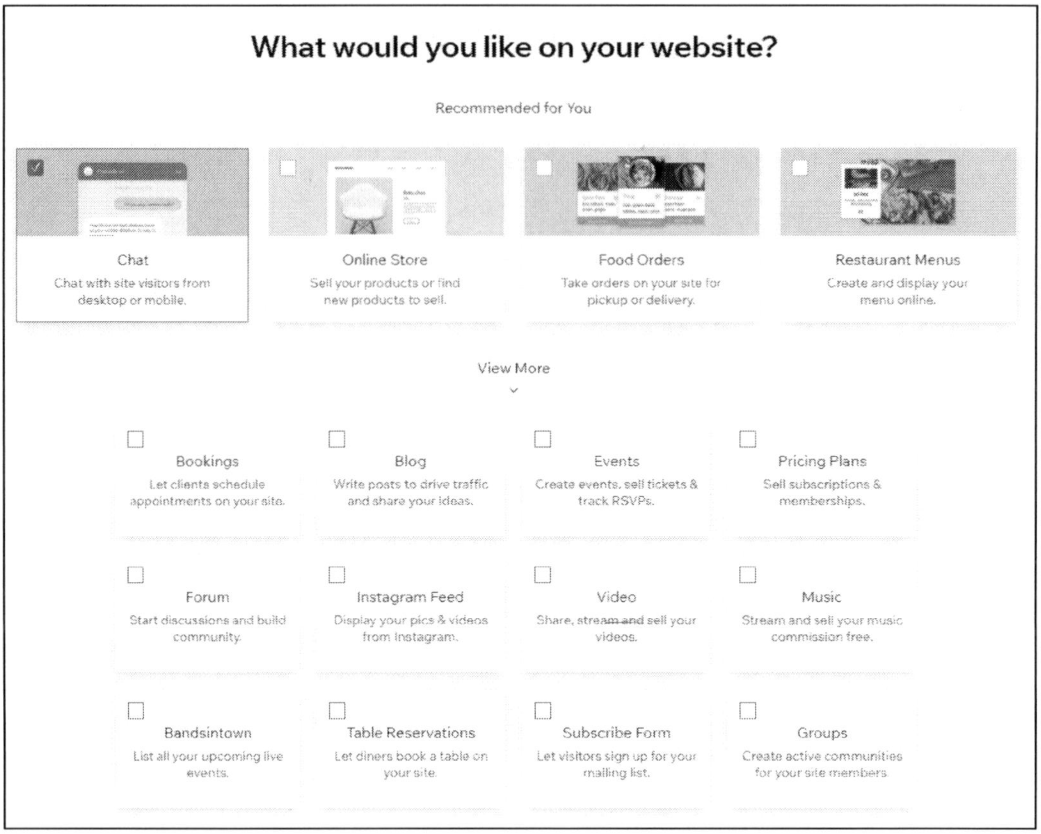

Figure 1.5

I will just leave everything unchecked and add features as I need them so I can show you how it is done.

Next, you will be asked about your website building experience and I will select *This is my first time* just in case this is your first time so you know what to expect.

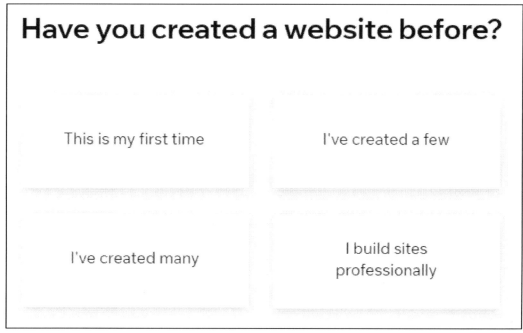

Figure 1.6

Selecting Your Website Type (Templates and ADI)

There are two methods you can use to create your website. Actually, there are three if you count starting from scratch with a blank website. But when you continue with the initial configuration after you tell Wix about your website building experience you will be given the option to either use the Wix ADI (Artificial Design Intelligence) or to use a template.

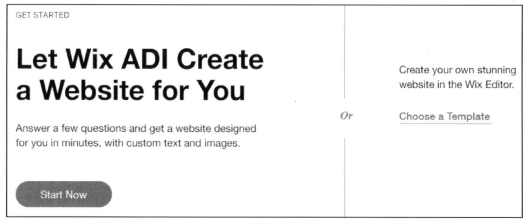

Figure 1.7

The Wix ADI will ask you some specific questions about your site and will use your answers to create a site template with the appropriate pages, images and layouts that it thinks you will want to use. Many people, including myself don't find this too useful but you can try it if you like and if it doesn't work out for you then you can go back to the default Wix editor and do things on your own.

Many people like to use templates because they are an easy way to get your site started and you can simply change the contents of the template to make it your own. If this is your first time using Wix I would suggest you do it this way rather than start from scratch because it will be easier to figure out how to use Wix because you can just change existing items rather than trying to figure out what to do with a blank canvas.

If you click on *Choose a Template* as seen in figure 1.7, you will be presented with several templates based on the type of website you told Wix you were creating. You can click on any one of the templates and choose *View* to see how the design is laid out to help you decide if you want to use that particular template. I will use the first one with the word Bread in the middle for my website by clicking on it and then clicking on the *Edit* button.

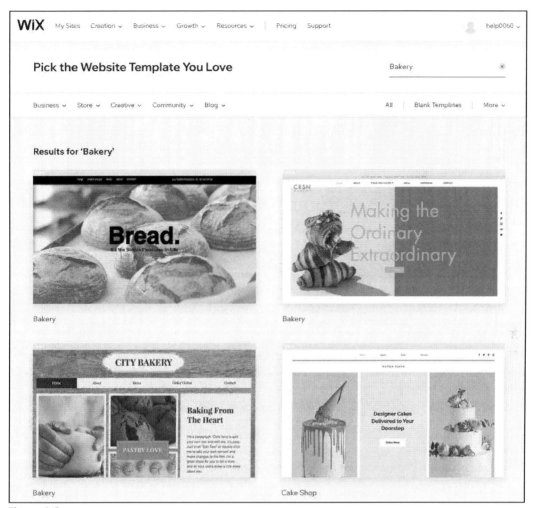

Figure 1.8

I will then be presented with the template I chose loaded in the Wix editor where I can then begin to customize the template to suit my particular website. You will be learning more about the Wix editor as you read on.

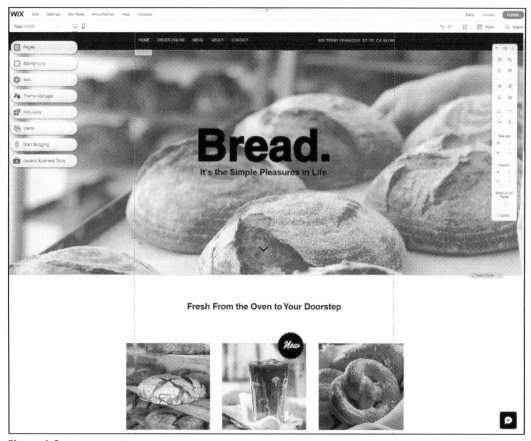

Figure 1.9

Chapter 2 - The Wix Interface

Before I start editing my website template I will first go over the Wix interface so you know what you are looking at when you first start working on your site. It might look a little overwhelming or complicated at first but once you start working with Wix you will find out that it's pretty simple and the tools and features you need will be fairly easy to find.

Wix Editor

The main workspace area that you will be working in is called the Wix Editor and it contains all the tools you will need to create your website. If you take a look at figure 2.1 you will see that there are various sections to the editor such as the text based menu items at the top left and top right, a toolbar over to the right, and then the main menu buttons to the left of the page.

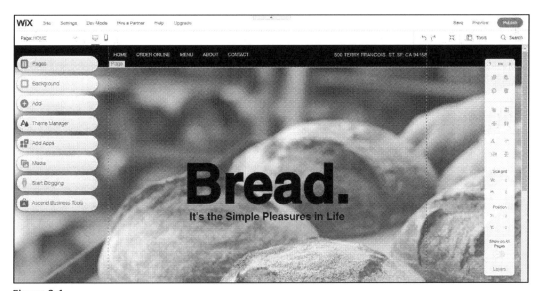

Figure 2.1

If you get in a bind and can't find a tool or component you are looking for, you can use the search box at the upper right hand corner of the editor to search for any features you might need. There is also a *Help* menu option at the upper left of the editor where you can search for help related to your specific question or problem.

At the upper right side of the screen there is also a *Save* option that you should use periodically to save your work just in case your browser crashes for any reason. Using the Save feature will not publish your website (make it live) but rather save your changes to your Wix account. When you save your site for the first time it will show you your Wix domain with the default my-site ending on it which you can change as I did in figure 2.3.

Figure 2.2

Get a Free Wix.com domain

https://help0060.wixsite.com/ triplecbakery

Figure 2.3

Notice how you can only change the ending of your domain address, but the beginning will have the username that Wix assigns to you based on the email address you used to sign up for your account. If you have a domain that you have previously purchased for this website then you can use the *Connect your own customized domain* option to use that instead of the free domain name.

Wix has an autosave feature that will be on by default so if you do end up with a computer issue then you might not lose as much work as you thought based on when your crash occurred. You can also turn off this autosave feature if you want to decide when your work is saved.

Now I would like to go into a little more detail about the specific components of the dashboard so you can get an idea of what tools are where before you get started. As I go along in this book you will get a better understanding of where things are located.

Text Based Menus
At the top left of the dashboard you have some menu items that you can use to do things such as preview or publish your site, connect your personal domain or set up your business information etc. There are only a couple of menu items you really need to worry about here.

Site Menu
The selections from this menu can be used to adjust general overall site settings rather than make changes to the site itself.

Figure 2.4

- **Save** – This is another place you can go to save your work.

- **Preview** – If you want to see how your site will look when it's published you can preview it here.

- **Get Feedback** – This can be used to get feedback from other people about your site. You can send them the provided link and they can add comments to your site for you to then review later.

- **Publish** – When you are ready for your site to go live you can publish it to make it publicly visible.

- **View Published Site** - Once your site is published you can see the live version.

- **Release Manager** – If you decide to have different release candidates for your site you can manage them here. Release candidates can be used to test out changes before making the changes live on the final version of the site.

- **Site History** – Wix will save various versions of your site as you work on it and if you want to review or restore one of these older versions you can do so from here.

- **Duplicate Site** – Here you can make a duplicate copy of your site in case you want to do things such as make a second version of your original but with different content.

- **Transfer Site** – This option will allow you to transfer your site ownership to a different person.

- **Move Site to Trash** – If you decide that you don't want to keep your site for any reason, you can delete it from here.

Settings Menu

I will be going over most of these items throughout the book and will have a section on Wix settings in Chapter 7 but for now I will just give you a brief overview of some of the more important tools from the Settings menu.

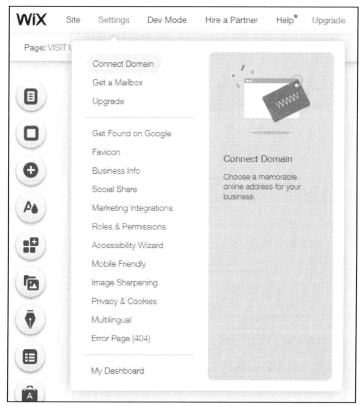

Figure 2.5

- **Get a Mailbox** – If you are planning on using your website for an online business it's a good idea to have an email address that corresponds with your domain, so it looks more professional. You don't want to use something like a Yahoo email address to sell you products or services.

- **Get Found on Google** – There are settings here that can be used to help index your site with Google so it will have a better chance of coming up in online searches.

- **Favicon** – Favicons are the little site icons that appear on the tab of your web browser for that page you happen to be on.

- **Social Share** – If you have a social media presence on sites such as Facebook or Twitter then you can set up icons and links so people can connect with you on those platforms.

- **Mobile Friendly** – You can use the settings here to help ensure your website will appear correctly on mobile devices.

21

Wix Toolbar

Off to the right side of the screen you will find the toolbar that has various shortcuts to common tasks such as copying and pasting as well as some not so common tasks that you will most likely end up using (figure 2.6). Many people don't find this toolbar too useful and if that ends up being the case with you, you can close it by clicking on the X at the upper left. You can also click on the dots at the top of the toolbar to drag it to a different location on your screen.

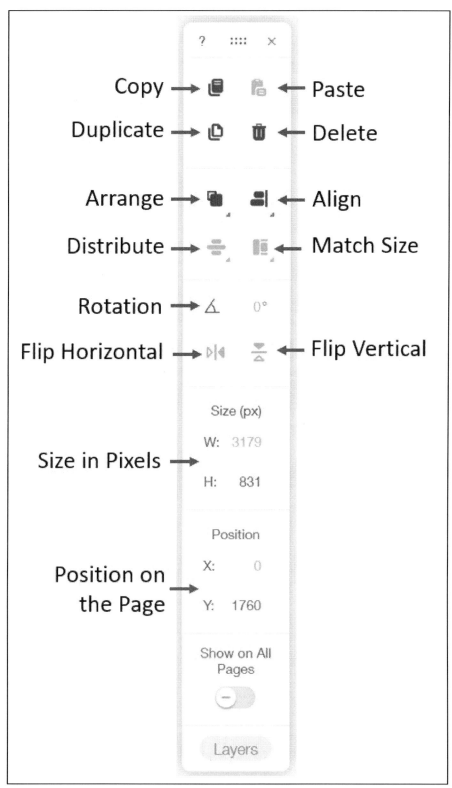

Figure 2.6

I will now go over the not so obvious options you will find on the Wix toolbar. One thing you need to keep in mind is that a specific tool will only be available (not greyed out) if you have an item selected on your page that the tool can alter.

- **Arrange** – If you have overlapping elements such as text on a picture and the picture happens to be covering the text, you can change its placement order using this tool.

- **Align** – This tool will help you align text or images etc. to the left, right, top, bottom, center or middle of the page.

- **Distribute** – This will allow you to distribute selected items on your page horizontally or vertically.

- **Match Size** – This will allow you to resize selected items on your page to be the same size as each other.

- **Rotation** – Here you can type in a degree of rotation for a selected item

- **Flip Horizontal** – Use this option to flip an image or other object horizontally.

- **Flip Vertical** – Use this option to flip an image or other object vertically.

- **Size in Pixels** – If you want to make a certain object an exact size and you know that size in pixels, you can type the number in the boxes for the width and height.

- **Position on the Page** – Here you can move an object to an exact location on the page rather than drag it with your mouse.

- **Layers** – Layers consist of all the objects on your page including images, text, strips (sections) and so on. Figure 2.7 shows what you see when you click on Layers from the toolbar. The items you have will vary depending on what page of your site you are on.

  From this box, you can rearrange your layers as well as click on the flashlight icon by one to have it highlighted on your page. You can also click on the eye icon to hide a particular layer.

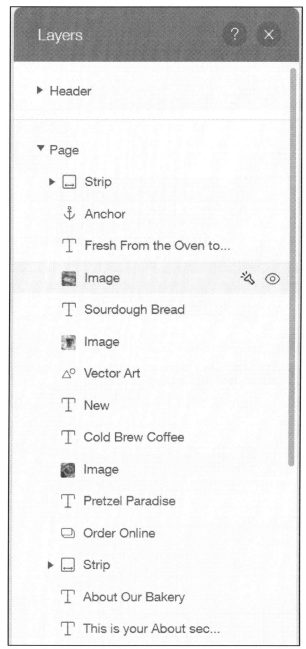

Figure 2.7

Main Navigation Buttons

On the left side of the screen you will have your Wix navigation buttons that will let you perform a wide variety of tasks on your website. You will spend a lot of time using many of these buttons and at the same time there might be some you never use.

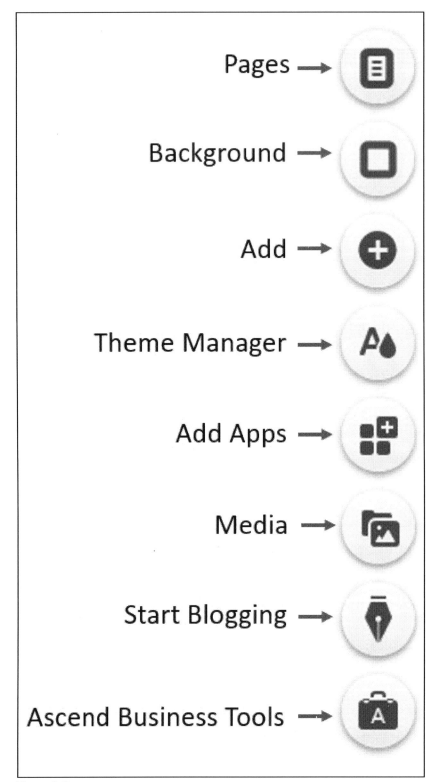

Figure 2.8

I will be using these various tools throughout the book so you will be learning what they as we go along but for now I will give you a brief overview of what each one of them does.

- **Pages** – Here is where you will manage the individual pages within your website. You can do things such as add new pages, delete pages, rename them, reorder them, duplicate them etc.

- **Background** – Here is where you can change your background to things such as a solid color, picture or video.

- **Add** – The Add section is where you will spend a lot of your time because it's where you go to add pretty much anything you need to your page such as text, images, buttons, forms and so on.

- **Theme Manager** – If you would like to adjust the colors of the theme you are using then you can do so from here.

- **Add Apps** – You have the ability to add additional features to Wix by adding apps which enhance its functionality. I will be discussing apps in Chapter 6.

- **Media** – This is another area you can go to besides the Add section to place images or videos on your site. You can choose pictures and videos provided by Wix as well as upload your own from your computer.

- **Start Blogging** – If you want to have a blog as part of your website content then you can add one from the Start Blogging area.

- **Ascent Business Tools** – If you plan on using your new website for your business then you will want to come here and check out how you can use the Wix business tools to do things such as configure SEO (Search Engine Optimization) and marketing strategies. If your website is just for fun or something more informational then you might not have any need to use the tools here.

Strips

Strips are a very important part of the Wix interface and are one of the most commonly used components of your page. You can think of Strips as the different sections that comprise a web page.

Figure 2.9 shows my page and two of the strips on the page. The first one has the word Bread with the bread in the background. The middle section with the three images is a white page background and the second strip has the image of the hand and the glass.

Figure 2.9

Your page can have as many strips as you wish, and they are very easy to add and customize so they fit the theme of the page. I will be going into how to use strips in Chapter 4.

 Be conscious of how many strips you have on a certain page. You don't want your viewers to have to scroll down an extra-long page to get to the information they are looking for or to the footer of your site. They might lose interest and move on if that's the case.

Rulers

If you are the type who likes to keep things proportional or a certain size on your page then you can enable the ruler to help you size your objects. When you enable the ruler it will be placed along the top of your page so you can simply scroll your page to where the object you want to measure meets the ruler.

To enable the ruler, you can do so from the *Tools* menu item at the top right of the page. You can also press *Shift-R* on your keyboard.

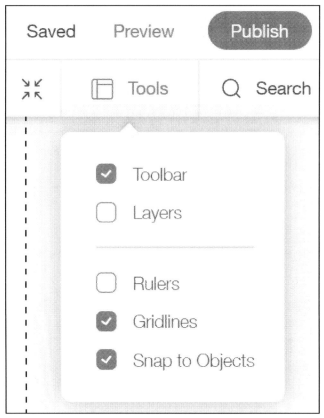

Figure 2.10

The ruler is transparent so it might be a little hard to see, especially when you have something like a busy image in the background.

Figure 2.11

One thing you can do if it's hard to see is zoom in or enlarge the page within your web browser. Many browsers will let you hold down the Alt key on your keyboard while scrolling your center mouse button to zoom. Or you can go to your web browser settings and find the zoom feature and zoom in that way. Figure 2.12

shows the zoom settings for Google Chrome as accessed from the three vertical dots in the upper right hand corner.

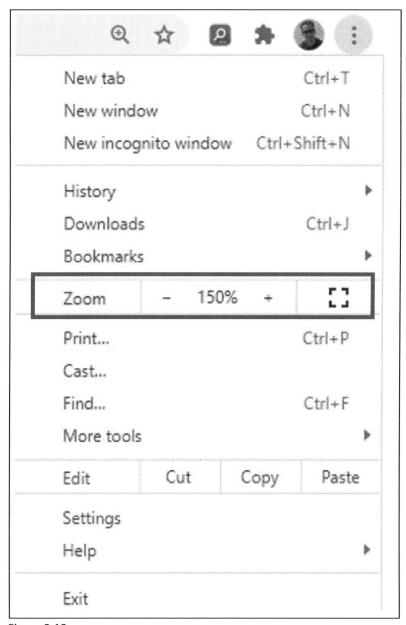

Figure 2.12

Gridlines

Gridlines are very important in the Wix interface because they are there to guide you when it comes to the placement of objects within your page. You will have a gridline (dotted line) at the top as well as the left and right of your page that is meant to guide you as to where you place your content. You should keep anything you want to be seen on your page within these gridlines.

Figure 2.13

As you can see in figure 2.13, my bread image goes past the gridlines and this is ok because this type of image is meant to be cut off if needed and if that happens, everything will still look fine. You can't really tell for sure how your webpage will look when it's live because there are different screen sizes and resolutions that people use on their computers and mobile devices and that will determine how much of your page will be displayed past those dotted lines. And no, the dotted lines will not show on your live page.

As you can also see in figure 2.13, the header items such as the Home, Order Online and Menu items are all contained within the gridlines. You should make sure you don't move these types of items outside of your gridlines. If for some reason you do not want to see these gridlines you can turn them off from the Tools menu.

Media Manager

As you can imagine, a website without pictures and videos is not going to be too exciting to look at. Thankfully Wix comes with many images and videos that you can add to your site if you do not like the ones that come with the templates. Plus one thing you might encounter if you use the provided images is that someone else might be using them as well and you don't want to have your website look like an existing site that is already live online.

If you plan on using your own images and videos, you can upload them to the Wix Media Manager so you can easily keep track of what files you have for your site and also place them within your site whenever you need them.

To open the Media Manager simply click on the *Media* button and then click on any of the links that say *Show More*.

Figure 2.14

Next, you will need to click on *Site Files* on the left to be taken to your personal Media Manager.

Figure 2.15

The first time you access your Media Manager it will be empty and you will see a notification suggesting that you start adding your files by uploading them to your

Wix site. You can either click on *Upload Media* and browse your computer to find your file or drag and drop them right into the Media Manager itself.

Start adding your files

Drag and drop files or upload from your computer.

+ Upload Media

Figure 2.16

Once you add files to your Media Manager you can then click on any one of your files and you will be shown detailed information about that file as seen in figure 2.18.

Figure 2.17

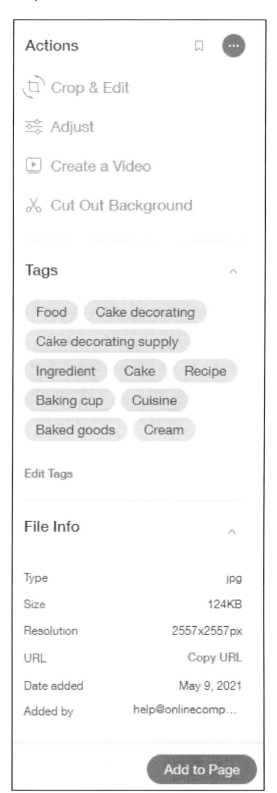

Figure 2.18

Here you can do things such as crop or edit your images as well as adjust things such as brightness, contrast and tint. You can even use the *Cut Out Background* option to make the background of your image transparent which is commonly used for websites.

 If you are going to be a serious website creator then you might want to look into some photo editing software so you can really make your images pop. Photoshop Elements is an inexpensive version of Photoshop that is easy to use. Check out my book **Photoshop Elements Made Easy** for easy to follow training. https://www.amazon.com/dp/1688736352

The *Tags* section is used for search purposes within your site, so you want to make sure that your image tags are accurate. Wix will add its own tags based on what it sees in your images, but you can add your own or remove any that don't belong.

The *File Info* section will show you details about your files themselves such as their size, type and resolution. You can also see when they were uploaded and by whom in case you have more than one user working on your site.

At the bottom of the image information section you will have a button that says *Add to Page* that you can click on to have your picture placed on to the current page you are on. Then you can do things like move and resize it to make it fit.

You can also click on the ellipsis next to a particular picture or video to get additional options as seen in figure 2.19.

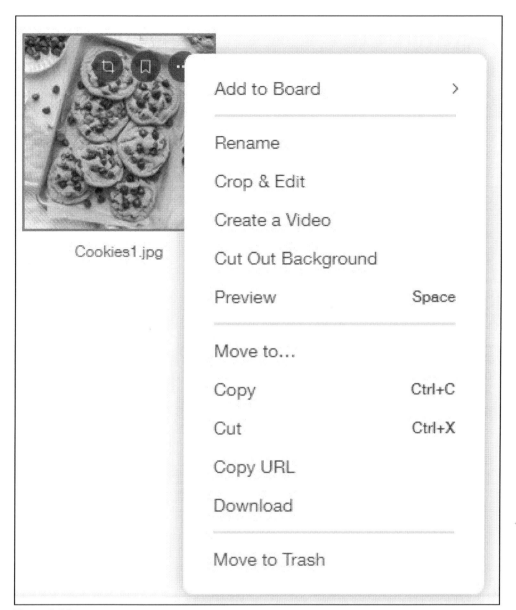

Figure 2.19

Chapter 3 – Creating a New Website

If you don't set up your new website when creating your account or if you want to create a new website in addition to any other sites you already have in progress or completed then this is very easy to do. I showed you how to choose one of the existing templates and also told you how you can use the Wix ADI (Artificial Design Intelligence) tool to answer some questions that Wix will then use to create your website template.

To see all of your websites in one place you can click on *My Dashboard* within the Settings menu at the top of the Wix editor.

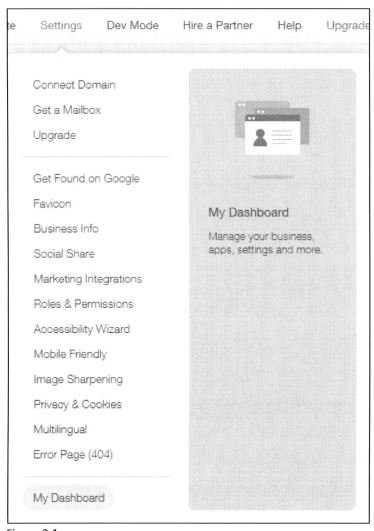

Figure 3.1

Then you would click on the *My Sites* dropdown from the Wix Dashboard to see the last site you opened. You can then click on *Go to All Sites* to see all of the websites associated with your account. From there you can view or edit any of your existing websites.

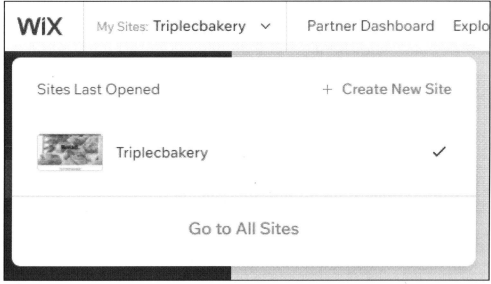

Figure 3.2

Creating a New Blank Website

To start a new site from scratch you can click on the link that says *Create New Site* as seen in figure 3.2. Then you will be asked to choose the type of website you want to create based on the provided categories. To start a new blank site you would click on the button that says *Other*.

What kind of website should this be?			
Business	Online Store	Music	Designer
Blog	Beauty & Wellness	Portfolio & CV	Events
Photography	Restaurants & Food	Fitness	Other

Figure 3.3

Next, you will be prompted to choose between the Wix ADI and using a template. You will want to click on the *Edit a Template* button.

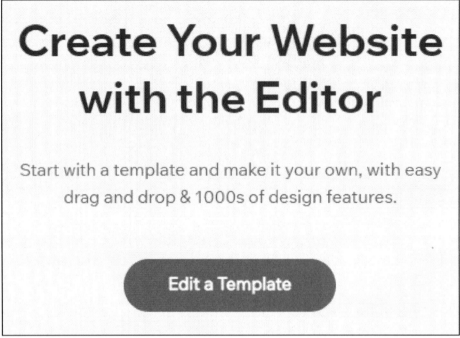

Figure 3.4

Next, you will click on *Blank Templates* at the top of the page.

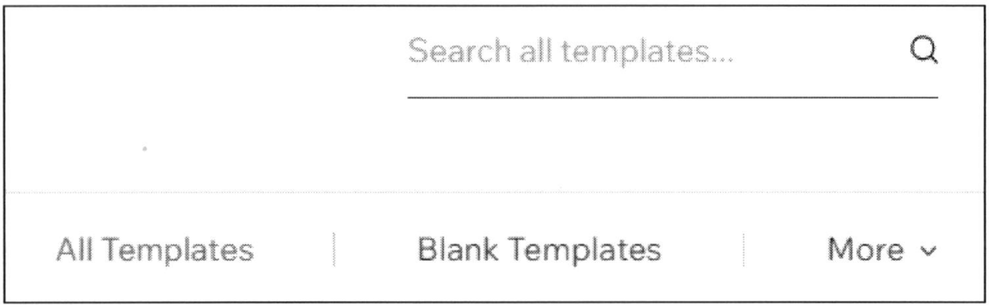

Figure 3.5

Now you can choose between a completely blank starting page (Start from Scratch), or you can choose some of the layout options which give you a starting point for where you can add your text and images without actually using any template design features like you would see if you used a regular template.

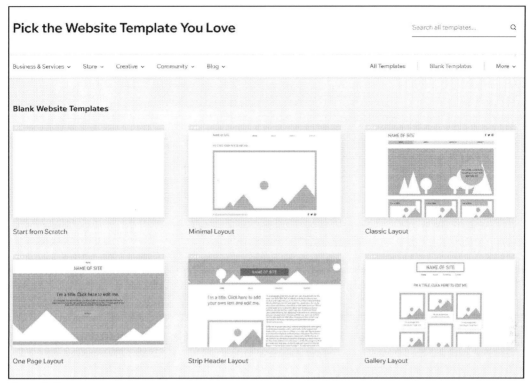

Figure 3.6

If I were to choose the Classic Layout option I would end up with an almost blank new site but have some sections created to help get me started as seen in figure 3.7.

Figure 3.7

Choosing a New Template

If you would rather stick with a preconfigured template for your new site then you can click on *All Templates* after clicking on *Other* for the website type to be shown all of the available template categories.

Figure 3.8

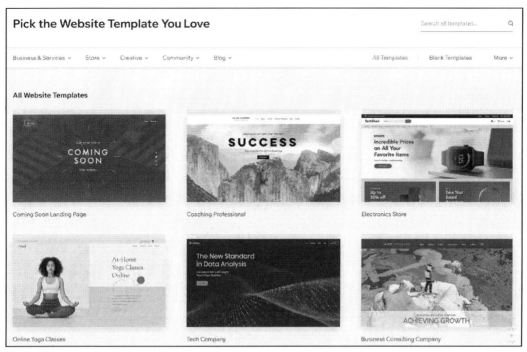

Figure 3.9

The templates are broken down into different categories such as business, stores, creative, community and blog with their own subcategories as well. This gives you a wide variety of choices when it comes to template designs. You can also use the search box to look for a specific template subject.

When you find a template you like, you can hover your mouse over it and choose *View* to see how it looks full screen or *Edit* to load the template into your Wix editor to begin working on it.

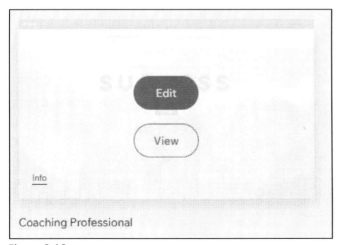

Figure 3.10

Website Preview
As you are working on your website, you will want to know how it will look outside of the Wix editor without all the toolbars and menu items. Plus you will need to be able to make sure that everything looks correct before you publish it and make it live for the world to see.

Fortunately, this is very easy to do, and you can preview your website any time you like to make sure that your changes appear the way you wanted them to. At the top right of the Wix editor you will see a link called *Preview* that you can click on to open your page in a new tab within your browser in preview mode.

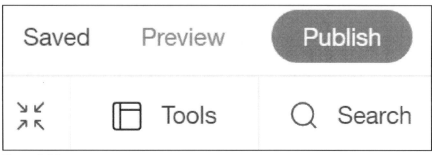

Figure 3.11

Figure 3.12 shows my website in preview mode and as you can see, the toolbars etc. are not shown. Figure 3.13 shows the top section of the window enlarged and you can read where it says *You're now in Preview mode* at the top of the page. When I'm done with the preview mode I can click on the link that says *Back to Editor* in the upper right hand corner to go back to editing mode.

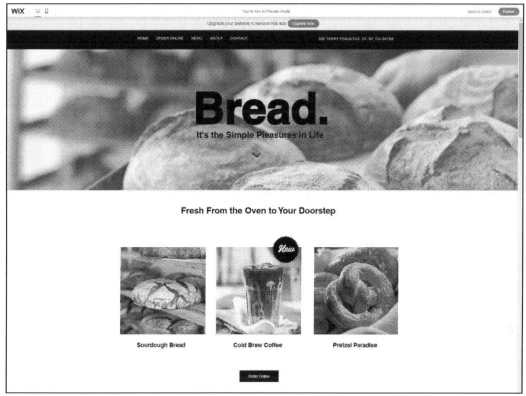

Figure 3.12

Figure 3.13

When you are in Preview mode you can use your website as if it were live. All of your menus and links will be active so you will be able to navigate around your site as if it were published so you can see how everything works.

To view your website in mobile mode you can click on the smartphone icon at the top left to toggle between desktop and mobile views.

Figure 3.14

The mobile view can be used to make sure that your site formatting choices will look correct on a mobile device. You can use your mouse scroll wheel to scroll up and down the page in the preview.

Figure 3.15

Chapter 4 – Adding Design Elements

Now that you have either a template or blank site in place, it's time to start adding things such as text, images and videos to your new page or edit existing items that came with the template.

Of course there is more to a website than just text and images but for some people, this might be all they need. Not everyone needs a complicated site with forms, blogs, events, animations and so on but if you do need these things, Wix can most likely take care of it for you.

I mentioned at the beginning of the book that Wix has more features than you will most likely ever use and to cover them all thoroughly would make this book a novel, but I will be going over everything you need to get up and running and hopefully by then you will feel comfortable figuring out some of the features I might not have covered.

The Add Button
One of the tools you will be spending a lot of time using is the Add button. This is where you will find most of the elements that you will be adding to your website such as strips, text, images, buttons, backgrounds and so on.

Figure 4.1 shows all of the choices you have when you click on the Add button and many of these choices will have subcategories and examples as shown in figure 4.2.

Figure 4.1

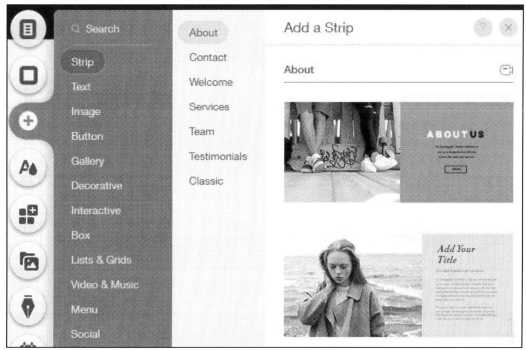

Figure 4.2

To add one of these elements to your page, all you need to do is click on it and it will then be placed on your page, ready for you to move, resize or customize.

Strips

One of the most common elements that you will be adding to your pages will be strips. Think of these strips as the individual sections of a page as seen in figure 4.3 where there are two image strips at the top and bottom over a white background. A strip can be a solid color, an image or a combination of both. If you want to add just a solid color strip you would find that in the *Classic* section, otherwise you can choose the style you want and then edit it as needed.

Figure 4.3

Once you choose the type of strip you want, simply click on it to have it added to your page. Then you can drag it wherever you like on the page and use the arrows to reposition or resize the strip as needed.

Figure 4.4

To edit a strip, all you need to do is click anywhere on that strip and you will have the option to change the strip background, add a scroll effect, change the layout (left, right or center), or have the image stretched across the screen.

Figure 4.5

Scroll effects are used to add animation style effects to your strips so when your page is live it will have a little more pop to it rather than just stay stationary. I would suggest applying different styles to your strip and then using the Preview mode to see how they look.

Don't go to crazy with styles and other animation type effects on your website because you don't want it to appear too busy and take away from the content of the site itself. You don't want your website looking like an overdone PowerPoint presentation!

When using images for your strip backgrounds, make sure they are the type that will look ok when they are cut off because how much of the image that gets displayed will be determined by the screen size and resolution of the device your visitors are viewing the page on.

Since my website is about cakes, cookies and cupcakes I will change my home page strip image to something more appropriate than a picture of bread. To do so, I will click on *Change Strip Background* and choose the *Image* option. I will then search for **cookies cake cupcakes** and will be shown the search results. I can then filter them by images from Wix as well as from Shutterstock and Unsplash. I can also filter by type, category and orientation.

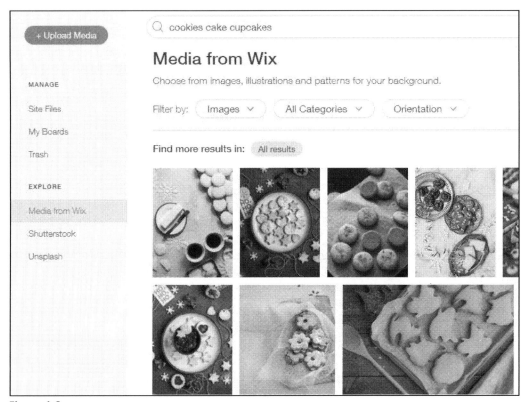

Figure 4.6

One thing to be aware of is that not all the images you find here will be free to use so make sure to look for the $ next to many of them because that tells you that you will need to purchase that image to use it. You also have the option to use your own uploaded images from the *Site Files* category. Once I find what I am looking for, I can select the image and click on *Change Background*.

Now that I have found an image that better fits the theme of my site, I have made it my strip background, changed the text and already my page is looking much more like one that should go with my (fictional) business.

Figure 4.7

Backgrounds

Most likely your entire page will not be made up of a single image or multiple images so you will need to have some sort of background between your strips or behind smaller images to help break things up.

Right now, my site template came with a white background between my strips that contain images, and this happens to work just fine for my site. But if I wanted to change this to a different color or even an image itself, I can click anywhere on the background and then choose *Change Page Background*.

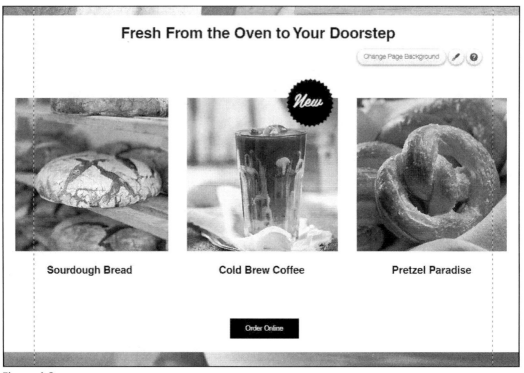

Figure 4.8

Then I will have the option to add a background image or video and also to change the solid color from white to another color of my choosing. If I find an image I like and want to have it on all of my other pages then I can click on the button that says *Apply to Other Pages*.

Figure 4.9

If I wanted to change the color, I would be presented with some colors that match the theme of my template so I can try and keep things looking uniform. I can also add custom colors or even type in the hex number for an exact color that I want to use.

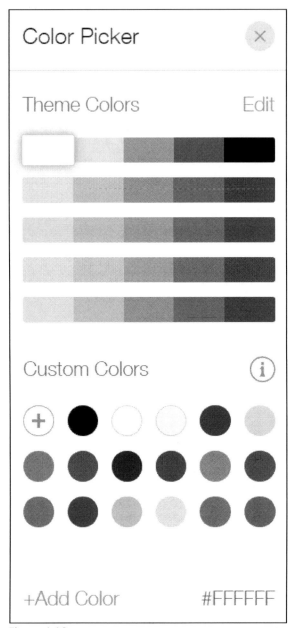

Figure 4.10

When adding images and videos to your site, keep in mind that some people may be viewing your site on a slow connection such as on the road with a mobile device, and it might take time for a large image or video to load and cause them to move on to another website.

Headers and Footers

If you have ever used a program like Microsoft Word or another word processing app then you might be familiar with the concept of headers and footers. Headers are items at the top of the page that usually contains information that you want to be repeated on every page.

If you look at figure 4.11 you will see that it has my website navigation for my other pages in the header section (home, order online, menu, about and contact). I want these items to be included on every page of my site so my visitors can get to any page from any other page they may happen to be on.

Figure 4.11

Footers are similar to headers except they are at the bottom of the page and will contain things such as your business address and phone number or other contact information. Figure 4.11 shows the footer that came with my site template, and it contains a subscription form where people can enter their email address to sign up for a mailing list.

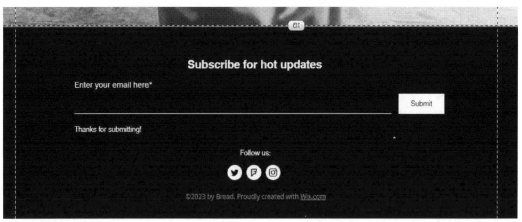

Figure 4.12

When you change the information on your headers and footers, those changes will apply to all of the other pages on your website. You can double click in your header or footer to change the design if you do not like how it currently looks.

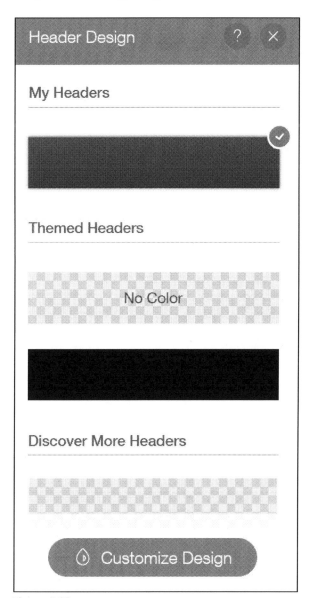

Figure 4.13

Adding Text

It should be fairly obvious that you need to have text on your website in order for your readers to know what the site is all about. If your site is just a bunch of pictures then most people won't find it too useful, and you might as well just start an Instagram account!

If you are using a template, you can easily edit the text on your page to make it your own style and of course change the wording, so it fits within the context of your website. You can also add new text as needed and format it to match your existing text.

To add text to your page, simply go to the Add button and select *Text*. You will then be presented with three different text categories with many choices within each category.

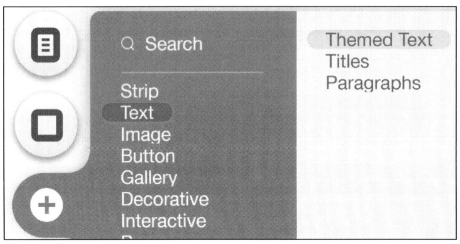

Figure 4.14

The type of text you should choose will be determined by where on your page you are placing the text. As you click on each category, you will be shown examples of the related text that you can then click on to apply to your page.

- **Themed Text** – These text samples can be used on different parts of your page and are based on the current theme of your page.

- **Titles** – Title text is commonly used on the home page for the main name of your business etc. Like in my case I have title text used for my Triple C Bakery wording on the home page.

- **Paragraphs** – Here you will find examples of paragraph styles that you can add to your page and then edit with your own text.

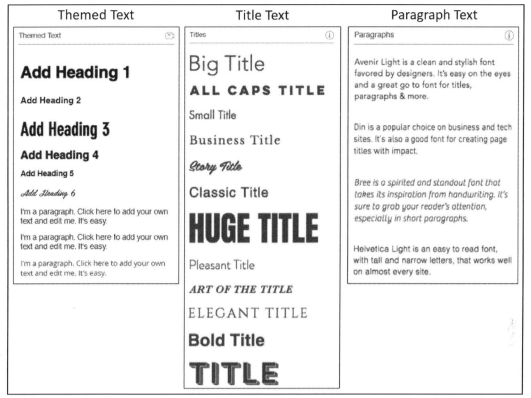

Figure 4.15

One thing to keep in mind when adding text to your website is to make use of the various heading text styles. Heading text is used to break up the content of your page and also to help search engines learn what your page is about by reading the text with the heading tags.

Heading text goes in order from larger (Heading 1) to smaller (Heading 2, Heading 3 etc.) and so on so try and break up your page contents using this type of text. You can think of heading text being used in a table of contents where there is the main chapter (Heading 1), and then subsections and other subsections within those sections.

Once you add text to your page you can easily edit the text by highlighting like you would on a document you might have open on your computer. Once you have the text highlighted, you will have many ways to format it as seen in figure 4.16.

Figure 4.16

Here you can change the type of font such as make it heading or paragraph text, change the font size itself, make it bold\italicized\underlined, change the color and so on. There are also options to justify your text to the left, right or center as well as create bulleted or numbered lists. You can also create links to other pages on your site or external pages using the link feature. I will be discussing links in Chapter 5.

The *Effects* section comes in very handy because it can be used to make your text stand out when it's over an image. You will often find that when you place text over images that have various colors and shading that some or all of the text will be hard to read. Adding effects such as shadows or outlines can often solve this problem.

Characters and Line Spacing can be used to stretch out your words by adding more space between each character. You can also use this to increase or decrease the amount of space between lines of text within a paragraph.

If you want to turn your text sideways you can use the *Vertical Text* tool. This can also be accomplished with the Rotation tool that you can find on the toolbar at the right side of the editor.

The *SEO and Accessibility* choice can be used to change the HTML tag of your text for search engine purposes. For example, you can change a line from an H3 tag to an H2 tag without actually changing the text itself. I will be discussing SEO in more detail in Chapter 6.

To move text from one spot to another on your page, simply click on it and drag it wherever you need it to be. Then you can stretch out or shrink the text box to make certain words be on the appropriate lines and adjust any line spacing as seen in figures 4.17 and 4.18.

Figure 4.17

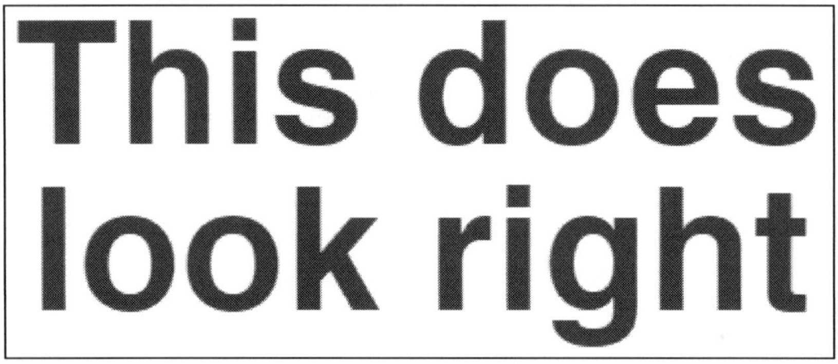

This does look right

Figure 4.18

Adding Images

Images are one of the most important aspects of a website because they are used to do things such as showcase your products or present a destination location and can keep your visitors on your page when they have something nice to look at. If you are using a template then it will have some nice images already in place, but you will most likely want to replace at least some of them to personalize your site.

Figure 4.19 shows the three images that were included on the homepage with the template I chose. You might have noticed that the images on the left and the right go over the dotted grid lines. This is fine and doesn't necessarily mean they will be cut off but overall you want to try and stay within these lines for anything that you really don't want to get cut off.

Figure 4.19

The *New* graphic is also an image, or I should say vector art with the word New added as text on top of it. You can add vector art the same way you do images.

Since my site is about cupcakes, cookies and cakes, I will replace each of these images with one from each category and also change the text at the bottom. This time I will use images that I have uploaded to my Wix Media Manager. Normally I would click on the *Add* button, choose *Image* and then select *My uploads*. But since I am replacing an existing image, I will select the first image and click on the *Change Image* button. Then I will select an image from my *Site Files* section and click on the *Choose Image* button.

As you can see in figure 4.20, Wix replaced the image on the left and even made it the same size as the picture that was previously in that location.

Figure 4.20

If I don't like the way it cropped my image then I can select it and then click on the Crop button. I don't like how it cut off the bottom of the cupcake so I will click on *Crop* and move the image around, so it fits better in the box. The results are shown in figure 4.22.

Figure 4.21

Figure 4.22

I will now replace the other images and change the text underneath each one. I will also need to change the color of the New vector from black to red, so it doesn't blend into the picture of the cake.

Figure 4.23

Next, I am going to add my company logo to my homepage and place it above the title text on my strip image. This process works the same way as replacing an image except Wix will add the image to your page without cropping it to fix a set space. Then you can simply drag the image to where it needs to go and resize it accordingly.

Figure 4.24

You might have noticed that my logo image has a transparent background meaning you can see through it. If it had a white or colored background it would not look correct on the site and look just like figure 4.25.

Figure 4.25

Wix will allow you to edit or enhance your photos within the app itself if you don't have your own photo editing software. You can click on an image and then go to *Settings* and then click on the *Adjust* button to open the Wix Photo Studio. Here you can do things to your images such as crop, resize, enhance, adjust various attributes, add a filter, add text and so on.

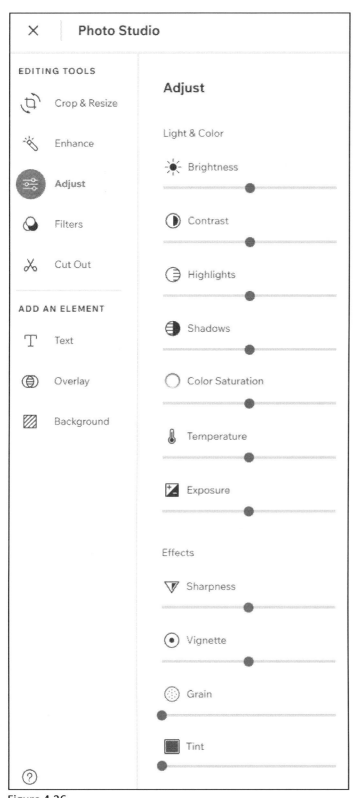

Figure 4.26

Buttons

One very common element you will find on many websites are buttons that are used to do things such as download files, send an email, add items to your shopping cart and so on. Wix makes it easy to add buttons to your site that you can then customize to fit the look and feel of your pages. There are a variety of included button designs and you can even add your own if you are the creative type.

My template came with an Order Online button already in place and linked to the included order page which you have not seen yet. If I click on this button I will have options to do things such as change the button text, its layout, the design and also the link that is tied to that button. Keep in mind that you should always have a link tied to your button otherwise when people click the button, it won't take them anywhere.

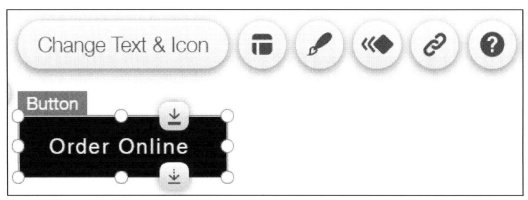

Figure 4.27

Rather than edit this existing button, I will delete it and then add a new one from scratch. Once again I will click on the *Add* button and then select *Button* and choose from one of the many button categories.

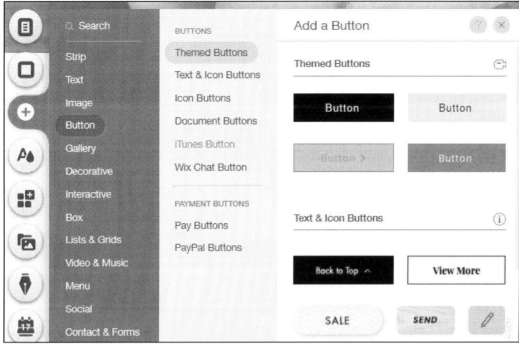

Figure 4.28

I have chosen a button from the *Text & Icon Buttons* section and placed it where the other button was previously located.

Figure 4.29

Obviously, I don't want my button to have the text that says Say Hello but rather want to have it say Order Online so I can change that as well as other design elements of my button by clicking on it and choosing the appropriate option. Clicking on *Change Text & Icon* will allow me to change the button text and also decide if I want my button to display text or just be a blank button. I can also add a link to my button from here. More on links in Chapter 5.

If I want to change other elements related to my button I can choose the *Design* option when clicking on my button. Here I can change the text attributes and button colors as well as add effects like shadows and custom corner shapes.

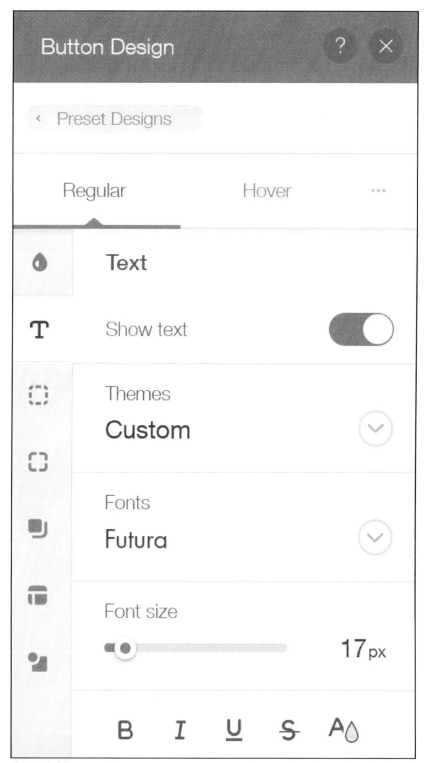

Figure 4.30

I will now change the text for my button so it says Order Online, change the font style and size and also add a drop shadow to the button itself.

Figure 4.31

Videos

Adding a video to your site is a great way to get your viewers interested in the topic of your website. It's also a great way to show off your products or highlight something like your rental vacation property.

There is more than one way to add a video to your site and you can even add videos from other sites such as YouTube. You can even have a background video on your page or strip itself to give your website that wow factor.

My template actually has video for the strip under the Order Online button. Of course you can't see the animation in a book but what it shows is the water pouring out of the glass into the flour and it just repeats over and over when you are on the page.

If I click on my strip, I will get the same type of options that you have seen when clicking on other objects. This time I will click on the *Change Strip Background* button and will see a menu as shown in figure 4.32.

Figure 4.32

From here I can click on the button that says *Video* to be taken to my Media Manager where I can then choose a different video for my strip (figure 4.34). Since the video provided by the template fits the theme of my website, I will leave it as is.

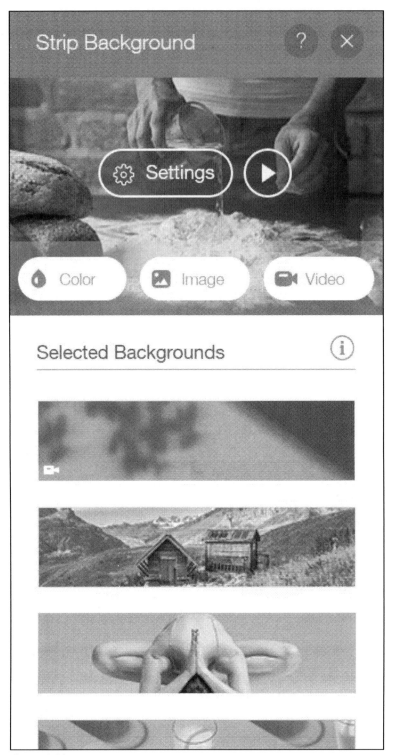

Figure 4.33

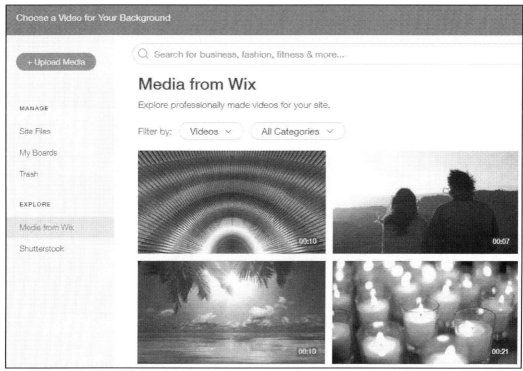

Figure 4.34

Now if I need to add an actual video that people can play and watch I can easily do so.

I had added a strip as an example earlier in this chapter (figure 4.35) so I will now edit that strip and remove the images and replace them with a video. To do this I will click on each image and press the delete key on my keyboard. I will also delete the text underneath each image.

Figure 4.35

After I removed the images and clicked on the strip I noticed that there were columns that were associated with each of the images. I don't want these columns on my strip since I am inserting a single video under the Meet The Team text.

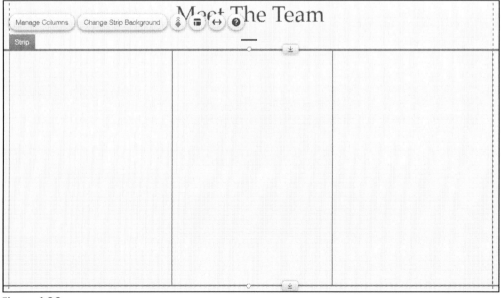

Figure 4.36

To fix this I will click on the *Manage Columns* button and then select each of the two of the columns and click on the trash can icon to remove them while leaving one that I will use for my video.

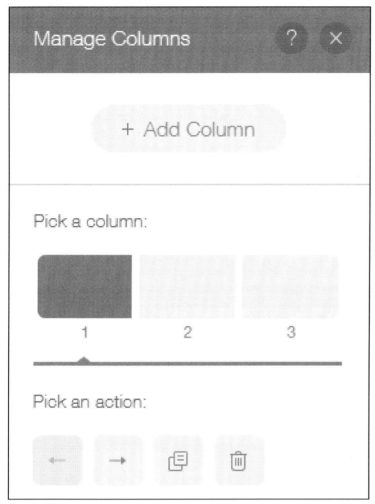

Figure 4.37

You have many options when it comes to inserting videos onto a page of your site. You can add an existing video from YouTube or Vimeo for example or you can upload your own video which is what I am going to do. To do this, I will go to the Add button, click on *Video & Music* and then choose *Video Upload* under the sample video.

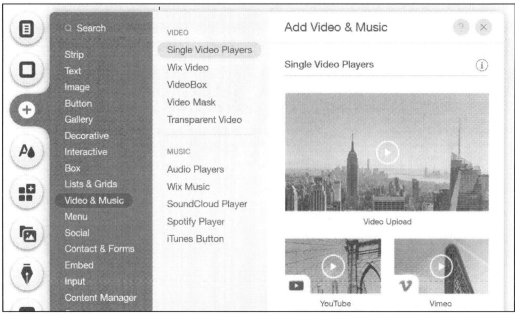

Figure 4.38

Wix will then add a video placeholder on your page that you can move wherever you like and also resize if needed. If you click on the placeholder you will have an option to change the video by clicking the *Change Video* button.

Figure 4.39

Once I click on Change Video I will have some options as to the source of my video. I will choose the first button which is to upload a video file from my computer. At the bottom of this option box, you can see that you can set the video to automatically play when a user visits that page and also to keep playing in a loop. I wouldn't do this because many people don't want to get bombarded with a video when they go to a website.

When uploading large files such as videos, be aware of how much space you are using in your Wix account. The free plan only comes with a small amount of storage space so you might find yourself running out of room rather quickly if you upload a lot of larger files.

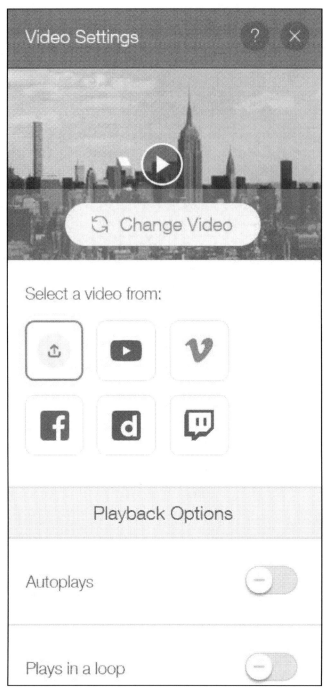

Figure 4.40

One issue you can run into when using the free account is that you can only upload videos that are 10 minutes in duration or less. If you try to upload a longer video you will get a message like seen below.

Upload Failed

Our Expert Bakers.mp4
Video duration 11:07 exceeds the free limit of
10 minutes

Figure 4.41

Now I have my uploaded video displayed on the page and when I preview this page I will be able to see how it will look when my site is live.

Figure 4.42

If I wanted to insert an existing YouTube video then I would choose that option and then add the video's URL (address) into the box, and it will then be displayed on my page.

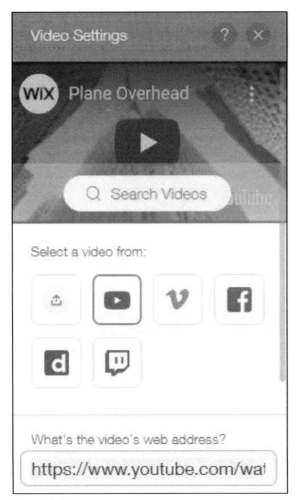

Figure 4.43

Object Animations

If you are the type who likes to add a little flair to your website then you can apply various animations to things such as strips, images and videos. To apply an animation, simply select the object you want to animate and then click on the *Animation* button.

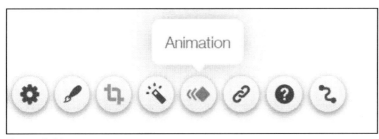

Figure 4.44

Then you can click on the various animation types and Wix will show you a preview of how it will look within the editor.

Figure 4.45

Clicking on the *Customize* button will let you fine tune the settings related to that particular animation such as the direction the animation happens or its speed.

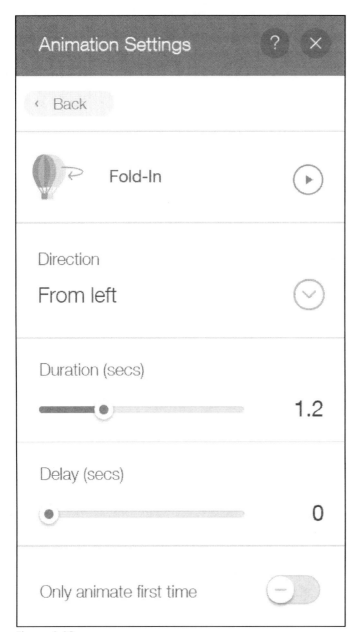

Figure 4.46

Right Click Options
Just like with most other programs and apps, Wix offers a lot of different options when you right click on various parts of your pate within the editor. The options you will get will vary whether you are clicking on a strip, image, background and so on.

Figure 4.47 shows the options when you right click on some of the more common types of objects. As you can see, you get many of the same choices on different objects such as copy and paste while other right click options are specific to the type of object you are clicking on. I suggest you take a little time and try out some of these choices to see what they do. Don't be afraid of messing anything up because you can always undo any changes you make with the Undo button at the top right of the screen or the keyboard command Ctrl-Z (Command-Z for Mac).

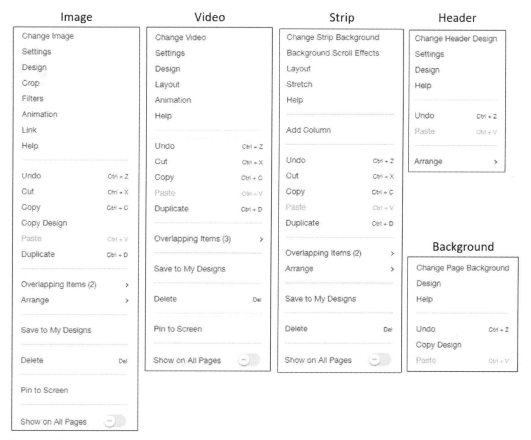

Figure 4.47

Chapter 5 – Adding Pages

A website with only a home page is not much of a website unless you have so little information that you can fit it all on one page. Most websites have several different areas or topics and each one of those areas usually needs to be on its own page.

For my bakery page, I have several areas besides the home page such as a menu page, order page and contact page. If I were to try and fit all of this on the home page, it would be very unorganized and also unappealing to look at. Fortunately, it's very easy to add additional pages as well as delete pages you might not need.

Adding and Managing Your Pages

If you started your website using a template then you will have more than just the one homepage for your site. You can view the pages on your site from the Page dropdown at the top left of the editor or from the Pages button at the top of the left hand navigation buttons. You can click on any of your pages to be taken to that page within the editor. You might have also noticed that the pages from the dropdown match the page name within your website header area (figure 5.2).

Figure 5.1

Figure 5.2

It's very easy to add pages and rearrange existing pages if needed within your website. To add a page, simply click on *Manage Pages* at the bottom of your page list and you will be brought to your Main Pages section where you can then click on the *Add Page* button.

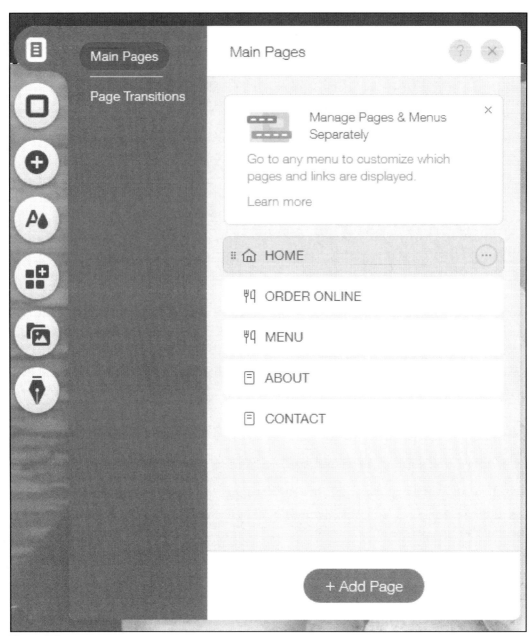

Figure 5.3

Wix will then add a new page under the page you happen to be on and then name it New Page unless you change it during its creation. If you want to rename the page you can click on the ellipsis (3 dots) next to the page name and choose *Rename*. I will rename my new page Visit Us.

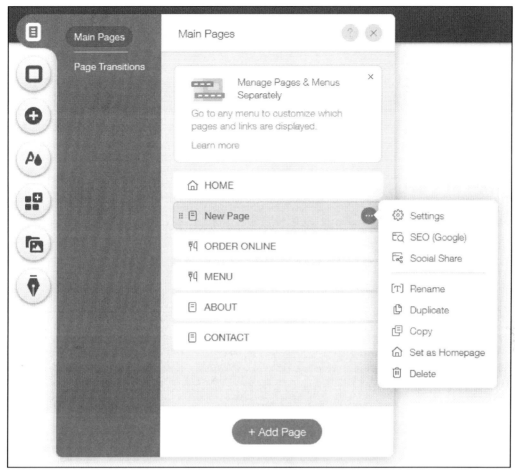

Figure 5.4

I will then drag my new page underneath my About page to change its order in my page list (figure 5.5). Then I will need to click on my header and choose Manage Menu and drag my new page to the position I want it to be at (figure 5.6). Figure 5.7 shows how my header looks after adding the new page.

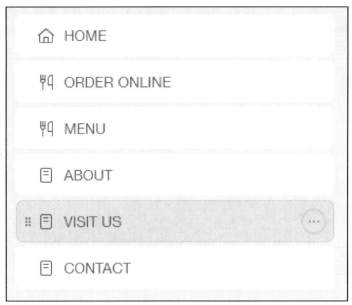

Figure 5.5

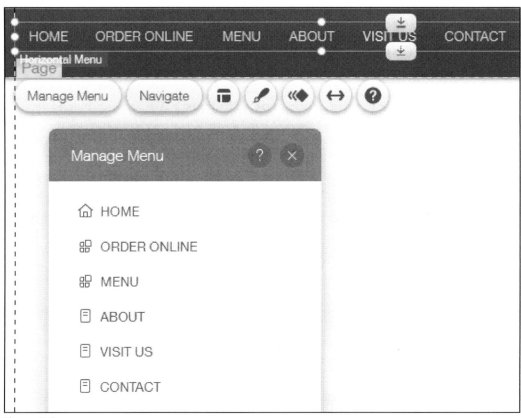

Figure 5.6

Figure 5.7

Subpages

Now what if I want to have my Visit Us page be a sub-page of the Contact page rather than its own menu item? To do this, all I need to do is drag the Visit Us page on top of the Contact page and it will become a sub-page of the Contact page.

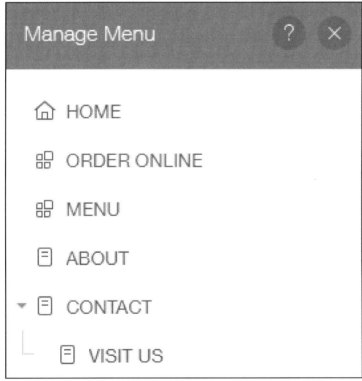

Figure 5.8

Now when I hover my mouse over Contact I will see my Visit Us page pop up underneath it, showing that it's a sub-page of the main Contact page.

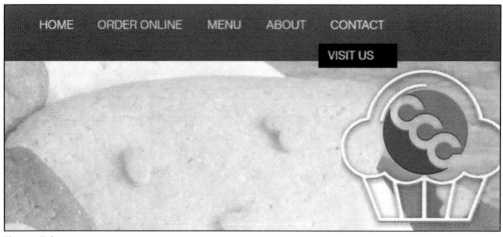

Figure 5.9

You can use subpages to keep your site more organized and also keep your header menu from getting too cluttered with pages that might not need to be shown there but that you still want accessible from the header menu.

Page Transitions

You can use the *Page Transition* feature to control how your pages are presented when your visitors navigate between them. These transitions are sort of like animations that happen right when someone goes to a page. There are not a lot of transitions to choose from and you also have the option not to use them if that is not something you want for your site.

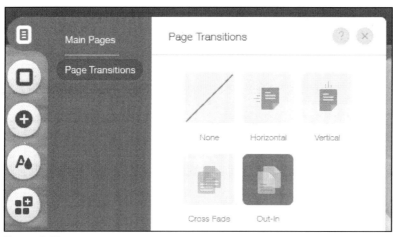

Figure 5.10

Just like with object animations, be careful not to overdo these page transitions as well because your website should be more about its content rather than how flashy it is.

Page Settings

Each page within your website has its own set of options that you can configure on a page by page basis. Clicking on the *Settings* gear icon for a page will give you a bunch of configuration options that you can change for that particular page.

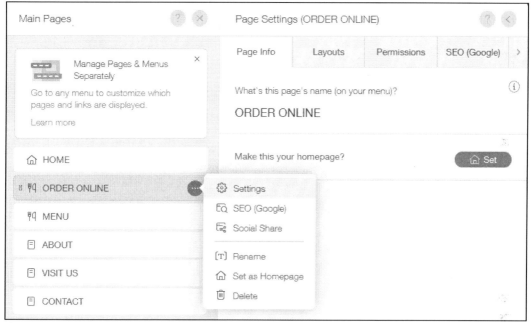

Figure 5.10

Here is what each section of the page settings will do.

- **Page Info** – This will tell you the name of your page and allow you to make it the homepage if it is not already.

- **Layouts** – Here you can choose to have a standard page layout with a header and footer or use a layout without these features if you do not need them on your page.

- **Permissions** – This will allow you the ability to control who can see this page. The default is everyone, but you can change it to password holders or members. I will be discussing permissions in more detail in Chapter 7.

- **SEO (Google)** – Search Engine Optimization is used to help to get your site discovered on search engines such as Google. I will be discussing SEO in Chapter 6, but you can change some of these settings from this section.

- **Social Share** – Wix has social media integration features and here you can add any images or text that you want to be shown when your page is shared on social media sites. I will be discussing social media in more detail in Chapter 6.

- **Advanced SEO** – Here you can add tags that are used by search engines to find information about your website.

Navigation Menu Management

The navigation menu in the header is where your listing of pages will be displayed, allowing your visitors to easily switch between them without having to use their back and forward button to go from page to page. If you don't like the default menu style or the design that came with your template then you can easily change the look with the available options you will have when you click on the menu itself in the editor.

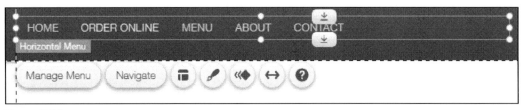

Figure 5.11

Clicking on the *Manage Menu* button will bring you to your page layout settings which you have seen before. I wanted to mention that if you need to hide a page from your navigation bar while you are getting it ready to go live then you can do so from here by clicking on *Hide from menu*.

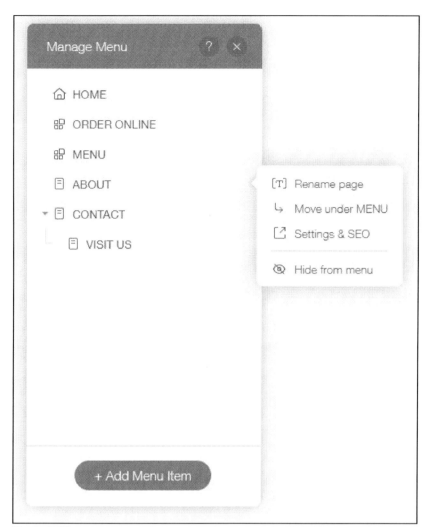

Figure 5.12

Clicking on the *Layout* button next to the *Navigate* button will allow you to make changes as to how your navigation menu looks as shown in figure 5.13. You can change the text alignment as well as having your menu items be shown from left to right or right to left. The section at the bottom that says *Show an item that says: More* is used if you run out of room on your navigation bar because you have too many menu items. You will then be able to click on More to see additional items. You can rename this to something else if you don't want to use the word More.

Figure 5.13

The *Design* button will let you change the look of your menu items as shown in figure 5.14. Clicking on the *Customize Design* button will let you change attributes such as text settings, fill colors, shadows and more.

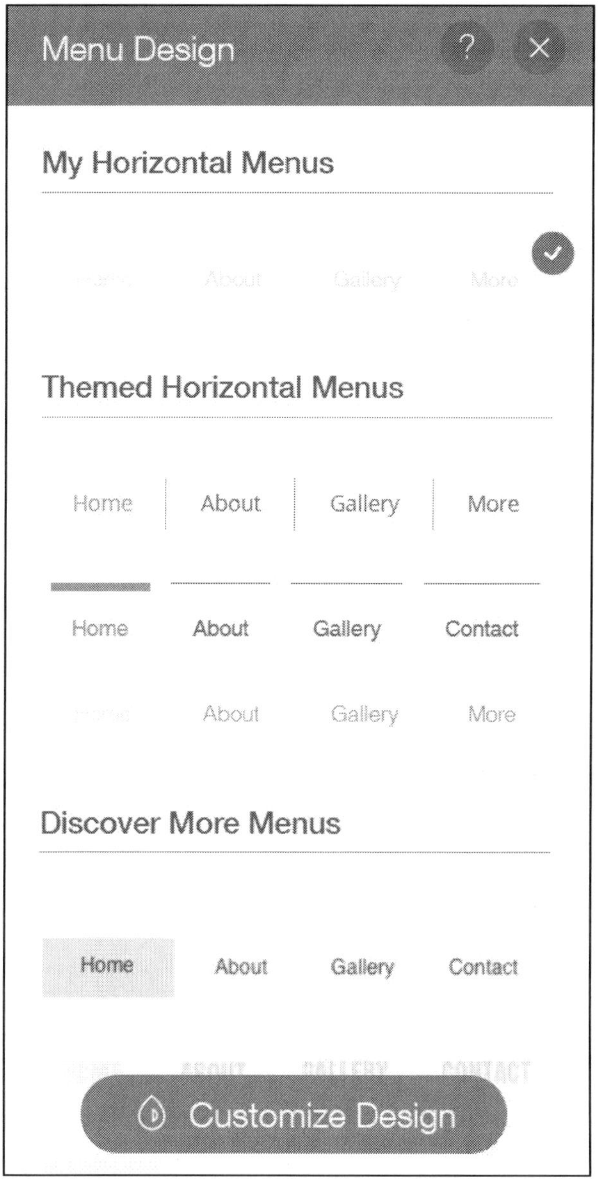

Figure 5.14

The *Animations* button will let you apply various animations to your navigation menu just like I discussed in Chapter 4. The *Stretch* button will expand your navigation menu to the edge of the page. Just be careful that you don't place your menu items too far to one side that they get cut off. If you look back at figure 5.11 you can see that when you click on your navigation menu, it will give you "handles" that you can use to stretch or shrink your menu as well as move it around the header section.

Right clicking on the navigation menu will give you additional configuration options as seen in figure 5.15. If you find that your navigation menu is not showing on all of your pages then you can come here and make sure that the setting labeled "Show on All Pages" is enabled.

Figure 5.15

Chapter 6 – Advanced Features

Now that I have covered the basic information that you need to know to get started creating your website, it's time go to over some of the more advanced features available to you in Wix that you can use to really customize your site. Keep in mind that I will not be covering all of the advanced features that are available to you so if I don't cover it here, it doesn't mean it doesn't exist.

Creating Links and Anchors

A website without links is not much of a website because without links, you will not be able to navigate to other pages on your site or to other websites. I was just discussing the navigation menu in the last chapter and all of the items in that menu contain links to other pages.

Going back to my home page to the Order Online button I created in Chapter 4, I can click on the button and choose *Change Text & Icon* to see the button settings (figure 6.2).

Figure 6.1

Since the section that says, "What does it link to?" says *Add a link*, that tells me that my button is not linked to any other page. To remedy this, I can click on the link icon and then choose where I would like to link my page to.

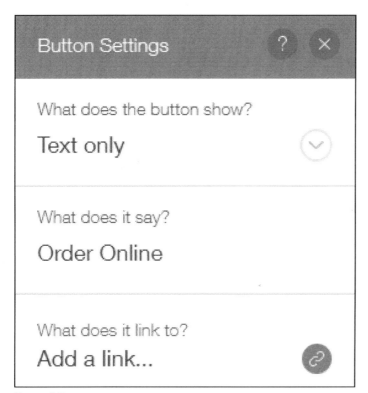

Figure 6.2

Since I want my Order Online button to link to my Order Online page, I will choose the *Page* option and then choose the Order Online page from the dropdown list. You have two choices as to how the page will open when someone clicks on the linked object. You can have it open in the current window which will replace the current page with the new page in your browser or you can choose to have it open the page in a new window while leaving the current window open (figure 6.3).

 What I like to do for my websites is to have links that are going to external websites open in a new window and have links that are going to other pages in my own website open in the same window. You don't want people leaving your page to go to another if possible and having the page open in a new window will keep them on your website as well.

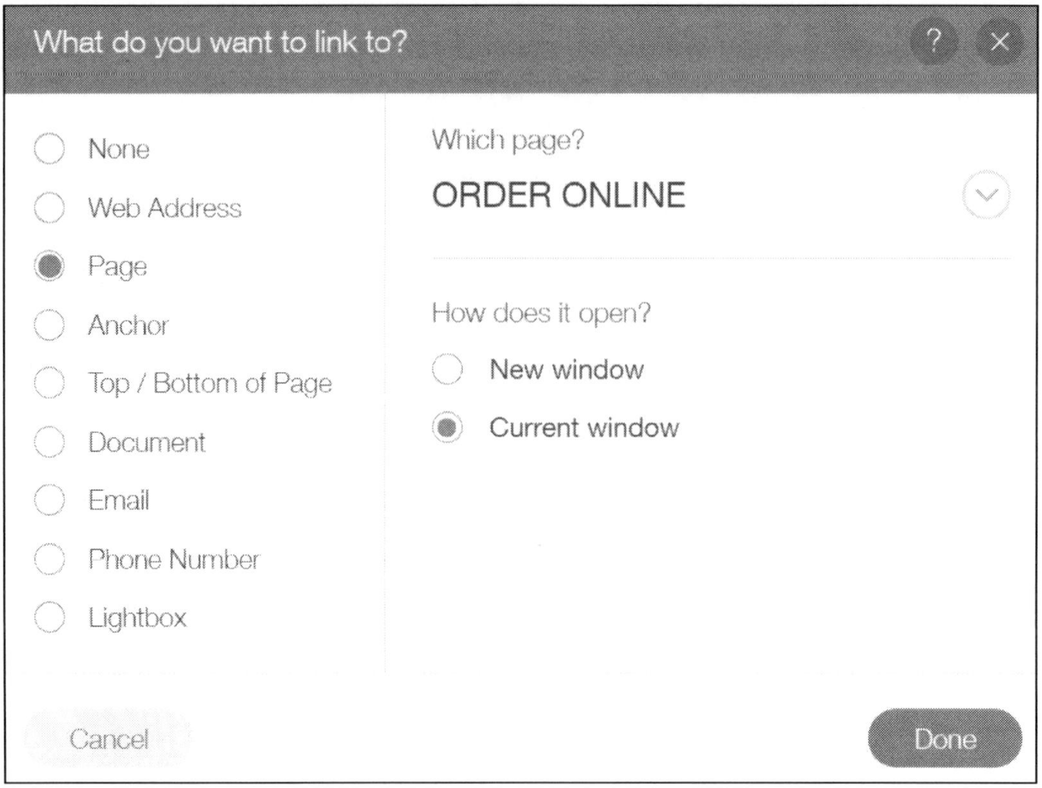

What do you want to link to?   ?   ✕

○ None

○ Web Address

◉ Page

○ Anchor

○ Top / Bottom of Page

○ Document

○ Email

○ Phone Number

○ Lightbox

Which page?

ORDER ONLINE   ⌄

How does it open?

○ New window

◉ Current window

Cancel   Done

Figure 6.3

Now I would like to take a moment to go over the other options from the link options from figure 6.3.

- **None** – If you want to remove a link from a page you can select this option.

- **Web Address** – Use this to have your linked object take your visitor to another website. You will need to type or paste in the address (URL) of the site you want the link to take them to.

- **Anchor** – These are used to take your visitor to a specific section of a page. I will be discussing anchors later in the chapter.

- **Top/Bottom of Page** – If you have a longer page and want a way to take your visitors back to the top of the page or the bottom of the page you are on then you can use this option.

- **Document** – You can have a link open a specific document that you have stored in your Media Manager. Just keep in mind that the document type you choose might not be able to be opened by all users or within a web browser so they might have to download it before viewing it.

- **Email** – This option can be used to open the visitor's default email program and have the email address you specify here entered into the To box of their client. This won't work for users if they don't have an email client configured on their computer.

- **Phone Number** – Many devices (such as smartphones) can dial phone numbers right from a link so if you want an easy way for your visitors to call you then you can choose this option.

- **Lightbox** – A Lightbox is used to show visitors some information such as discount codes or give them an option to join a mailing list. Use these sparingly because many people get annoyed when they see them and might end up leaving your website.

Figure 6.4

When clicking on other objects such as images, you can click the *Link* button to configure links to those objects. Or for objects such as text, you will need to click the *Edit Text* button to find the link settings.

Figure 6.5

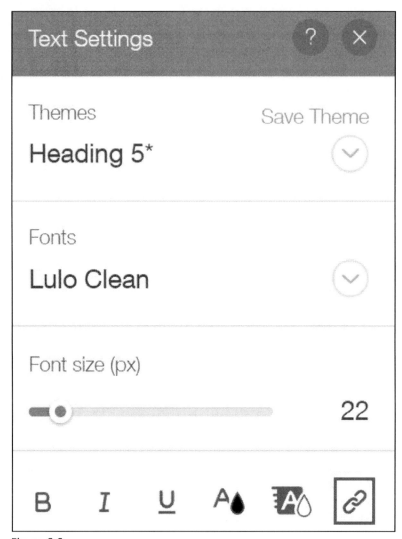

Figure 6.6

Anchors

Anchors are a type of link but rather than take you to a different website, they will take you to a specific area on a page.

Let's say I have some text that describes my bakery and I want to have a way to bring the reader to my subscribe area that is located at the bottom of my page in the footer. To do this, I will first need to highlight the text that I want to contain the link and then click on the *Edit Text* button.

Figure 6.7

Next, I will click on the *Link* button and choose *Anchor* for the type and then I can choose an existing anchor if I have any or choose *Add New Anchor* which is what I will need to do for my example.

What do you want to link to?

○ None
○ Web Address
○ Page
◉ Anchor
○ Top / Bottom of Page
○ Document
○ Email
○ Phone Number
○ Lightbox

Link to an Anchor

Visitors that click this element will go directly to the anchor on the page. Learn more

Which page?

HOME (This)

Which anchor on this page?

Order Online

Order Online

Add New Anchor

Cancel

Figure 6.8

I will then be shown a green line with the word Anchor that I can drag to the location on my page where I want my visitors to be taken when they click on the link I am creating in my paragraph from figure 6.7. I will drag the Anchor line down to the subscribe section at the bottom of the page. Since I want my anchor to be for the footer section I will drag it as low as I can go but will not be able to drag it into the footer itself.

Subscribe for hot updates

Enter your email here*

Submit

Thanks for submitting!

Follow us:

Figure 6.9

Now I need to give my anchor a name and will call mine *Subscribe*.

Figure 6.10

Now I can see that the anchor itself is called subscribe making it easy for me to tell what its purpose is.

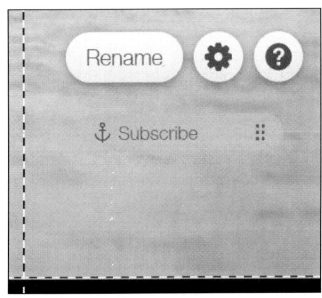

Figure 6.11

Now the next time I create an anchor I will be able to use that same one because it will show up in my list of anchors that I have previously created.

What do you want to link to?
None
Web Address
Page
Anchor
Top / Bottom of Page
Document
Email
Phone Number
Lightbox
Cancel
Link to an Anchor
Visitors that click this element will go directly to the anchor on the page. Learn more
Which page?
HOME (This)
Which anchor on this page?
Order Online
Order Online
Subscribe
Add New Anchor

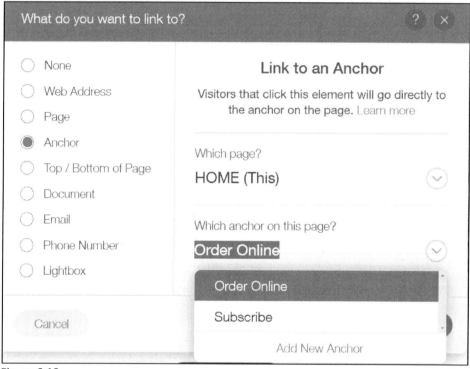

Figure 6.12

Now when visitors click on the word *subscribe* in my About Our Bakery section they will be taken to the bottom of the page right to the Subscribe box where they can sign up for email updates.

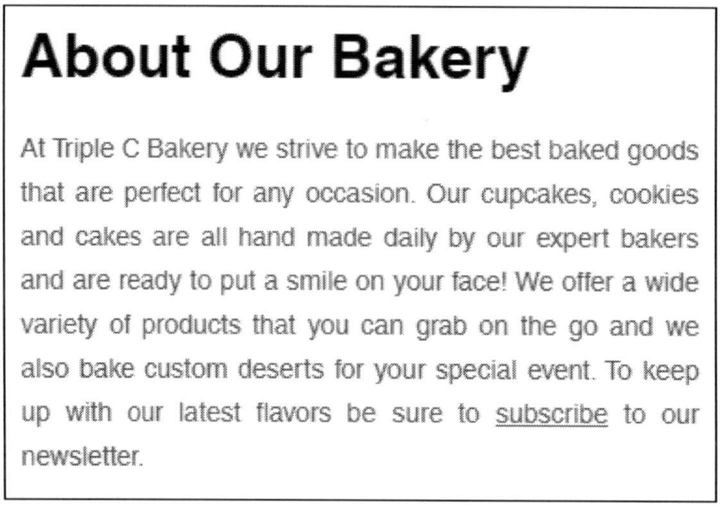

About Our Bakery
At Triple C Bakery we strive to make the best baked goods that are perfect for any occasion. Our cupcakes, cookies and cakes are all hand made daily by our expert bakers and are ready to put a smile on your face! We offer a wide variety of products that you can grab on the go and we also bake custom deserts for your special event. To keep up with our latest flavors be sure to subscribe to our newsletter.

Figure 6.13

Site Favicon

You might have noticed when you are going to your favorite websites that they have their own logos at the top of the page or on the tab itself. These are called favicons and figure 6.13 shows some examples for Amazon, eBay, Wix and Facebook.

Figure 6.14

Wix will let you add your own favicon to your website based on any image you wish to use. To add a favicon image you can click on the *Settings* menu and then choose *Favicon*. There is a catch when it comes to adding your own favicon and that is you will need to have one of the premium plans that include that option.

Figure 6.15

If you decide to upgrade to a premium plan then you can upload your image and Wix will then use it for your website. The optimum size for your favicon is 16x16 pixels which is a very small image size. The recommended file types are JPEG and PNG. I recommend using a PNG because you can make the background transparent unless of course you prefer to have a background in your image.

If you find that your image does not work well as a favicon, you can come back and either change it or remove it. If you don't use your own favicon, then Wix will use its own logo for your site.

Figure 6.16

Slider Image Gallery

Besides adding standalone images to your pages, you can also add slider image galleries which are pictures that move in a slide show fashion and allow you to display multiple images in one location on a page. You can also add collage type image galleries, but the slider type takes up less room and is a little more interactive but of course you can use whichever type works best for you!

To add a slider gallery, go to the *Add* menu and then to *Gallery* and you will see a *Slider Galleries* section with a few different types to choose from. I will choose the type where the images go inside the circles that will then scroll across the page showing the different images in my gallery. But first I will add a new black strip on my page for the background for my gallery.

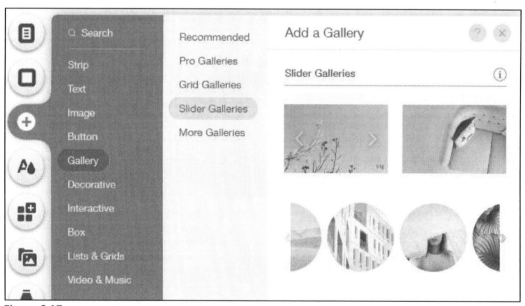

Figure 6.17

Once I have my slider gallery in place, I will need to edit it to remove the sample images and then add my own. To do this, I will select the gallery and then click on the *Change Images* button.

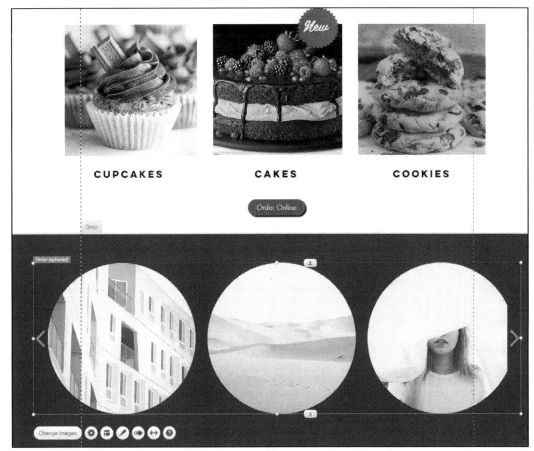

Figure 6.18

I can then either select the sample images and delete them or click on the *Replace Image* button to replace them with different images. I will delete all of the samples first and then add my own images by clicking on the *Add Images* button.

Figure 6.19

I will then select the pictures I want to use for my image gallery from my Media Manager and click on the *Add to Gallery* button. Then I will click the *Done* button and my new images will be added to my gallery and ready to go.

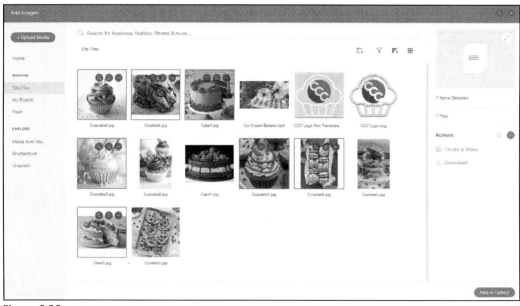

Figure 6.20

Figure 6.21

If I click on the *Settings* button for my gallery I can tell Wix how my images are to be displayed in regards to if they play in a continuous loop and also what speed the images will rotate. I can also change my images from here if needed.

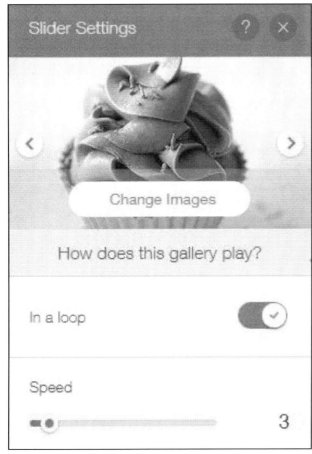

Figure 6.22

Social Tools

We all know that everything is about sharing and social media these days so it's almost a requirement that you have some sort of social media accounts to promote your products or services.

Wix has several ways that you can add your social media accounts to your website, and you can also customize them as needed. If you click on the *Add* button and then go to *Social* you will see that there are several options for various social media platforms.

Figure 6.23

I will be adding a Social Bar to the top of my About page so I will choose one of the options from the Add menu to begin with.

Figure 6.24

Once I have the social media icons in place, I will need to click on the *Set Social Links* button to add the site addresses for my various accounts.

Figure 6.25

From here I can remove any of the social media account types that I don't use and for the others I can type or paste in the address for my accounts in the section that says *What social page does this icon link to?* I will remove the Pinterest and Tumblr icons since I won't be using them. You can also add your own custom images if you don't want to use the defaults.

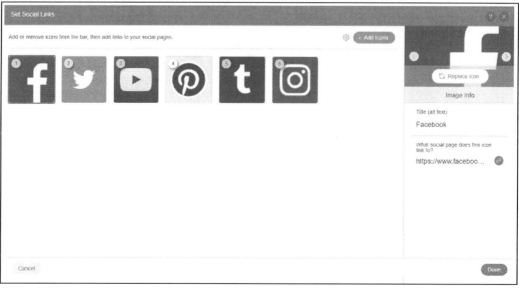

Figure 6.26

Since the space the social media icons take is now smaller, I decided to move them into my header next to my navigation menus.

Figure 6.27

When you place text or images etc. into your header section, it will get placed on every page of your website since that is what the header is used for. So if you want an object only to be on a certain page, be sure not to place it in the header area.

Embedding Objects

You might have noticed that many of the websites you go to have content from other sites or online applications built into that particular website. For example, you might go to a certain website that has a built in Twitter or Facebook feed that is updated in real time.

These kinds of page addons are examples of embedded content and Wix will allow you to embed a variety of content on your website. To see what is available you can click on the *Add* button and then choose the *Embed* option. Here you will see a variety of categories with different object types that you can add to your website.

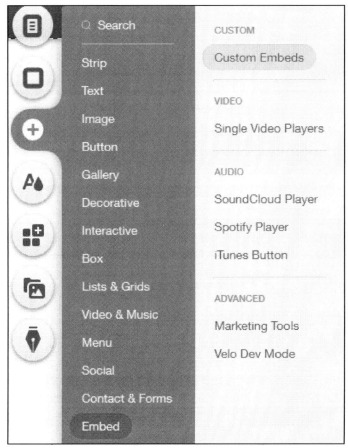

Figure 6.28

I mentioned adding a YouTube video to your site and that is actually an example of embedding content on a page. The process for embedding content on a page will vary depending on what you are trying to do. I will go through one example and show you how to embed your Twitter feed on your page so you can see how the process works.

First I will choose the Instagram Stream option from the Embed list. As you can see, it has options for Facebook, Twitter, Pinterest and YouTube etc.

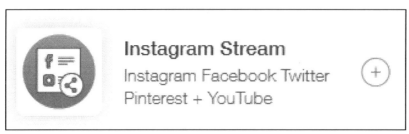

Figure 6.29

Next, I will need to click the *Add to Site* button and Wix will add the Social Stream app to my page.

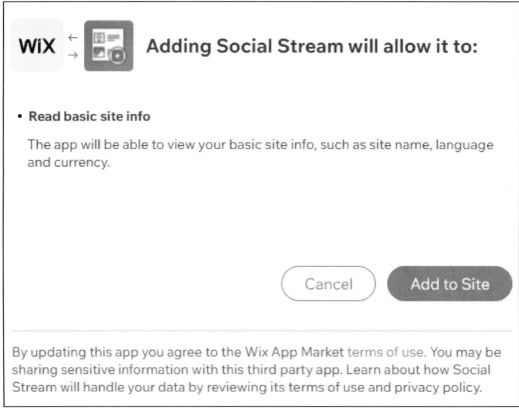

Figure 6.30

Now I will need to click on the *Settings* button for the POWR app to configure my Twitter account settings.

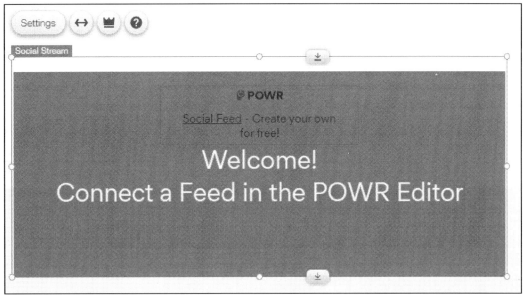

Figure 6.31

Next, I will click on the *Add Feed* button to choose the type of account I wish to configure.

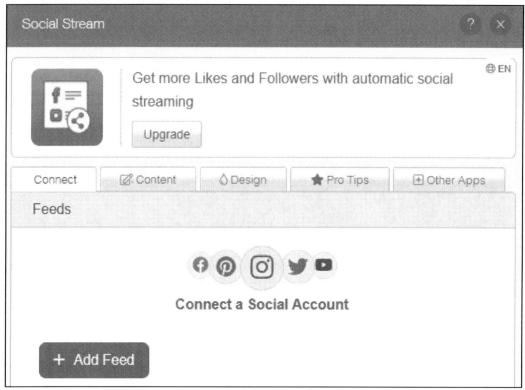

Figure 6.32

From the dropdown list where it says *Choose Your Social Platform,* I will select Twitter and type in my username which is OnlineCompTips. I don't have a Twitter account for my fictional bakery so I will be using my computer help site account for my example. You will also notice how this app will only show the 6 most recent tweets from your account.

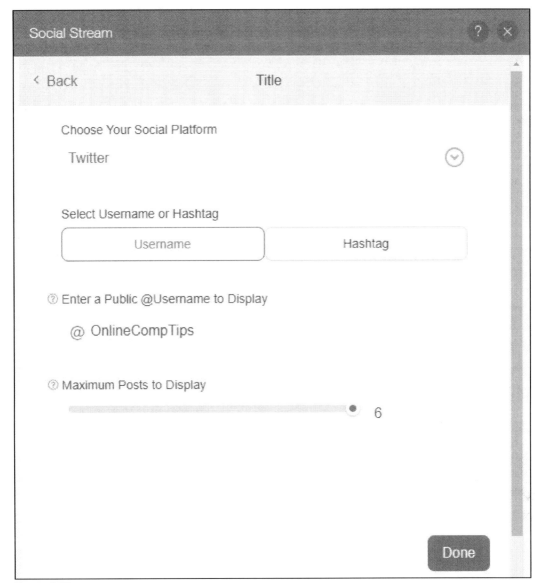

Figure 6.33

Now you can see that my Twitter account has been configured and is now listed in my *Feeds* section. If I want to remove it then I can click the trash can icon next to my username. You can also see that the free plan for this app only allows you to use two social media accounts on your site.

Figure 6.34

Figure 6.35 shows how my Twitter feed looks on my website and also how it shows the six most recent posts. I can also move this embedded object around the page and resize it if needed. If I don't want it there anymore then I can delete it just like I can with any other object.

Figure 6.35

Contact Forms

If you are planning on selling products on your site or providing services to people then you might want to have a way for them to contact you if they have questions. We all know that people don't like talking to other people these days and would rather send messages so this might be the way to go for your site!

Just like with everything else, Wix makes it simple to add a contact form to your site and you can have one up and running in just a few minutes. If you are using a template then there is a good chance that you will already have a contact form in place and you can then edit the form if needed. My template came with a form but I will add one from scratch so you can see how it is done.

The first step is to choose a place for your contact form. If you have a contact us page then that is a great place to put it. You may also want to add a new strip if needed to place the form on.

Once again you will go to the *Add* button and choose *Contact & Forms* and you will see that you have many different types of forms to choose from. I will go to the *Contact* section and choose the first form type from there.

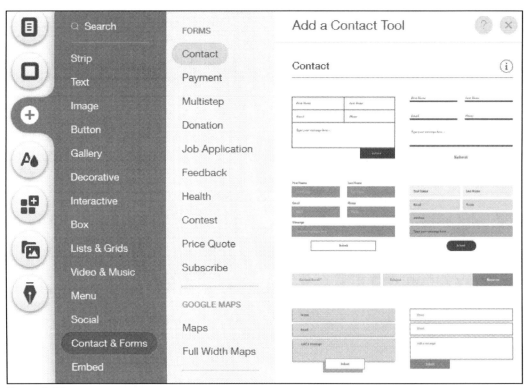

Figure 6.36

Now that I have my form in place, I will select it and click on the Form Settings button to see what configuration options I have for this form.

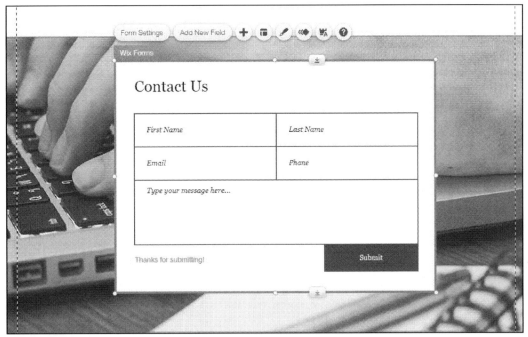

Figure 6.37

As you can see in figure 6.38, there are many settings you can adjust when adding a contact form to your page.

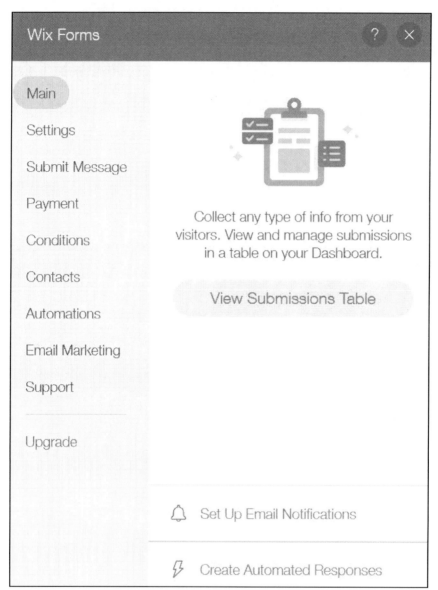

Figure 6.38

I won't go through all the possible form settings but will go over the ones that you need to check out to make sure your form is working correctly.

The first one you should check is under Settings and then Email Notifications. Here you should make sure that the email address you want your form submissions sent to is correct. You can also add additional email addresses if needed. By default, Wix will use the email address associated with your account.

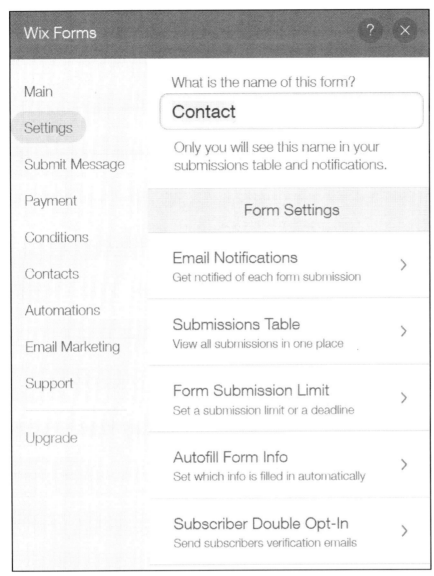

Figure 6.39

You might also want to configure the response your visitors will see after they click on the Submit button after filling out your form. This can be found under the *Submit Message* settings.

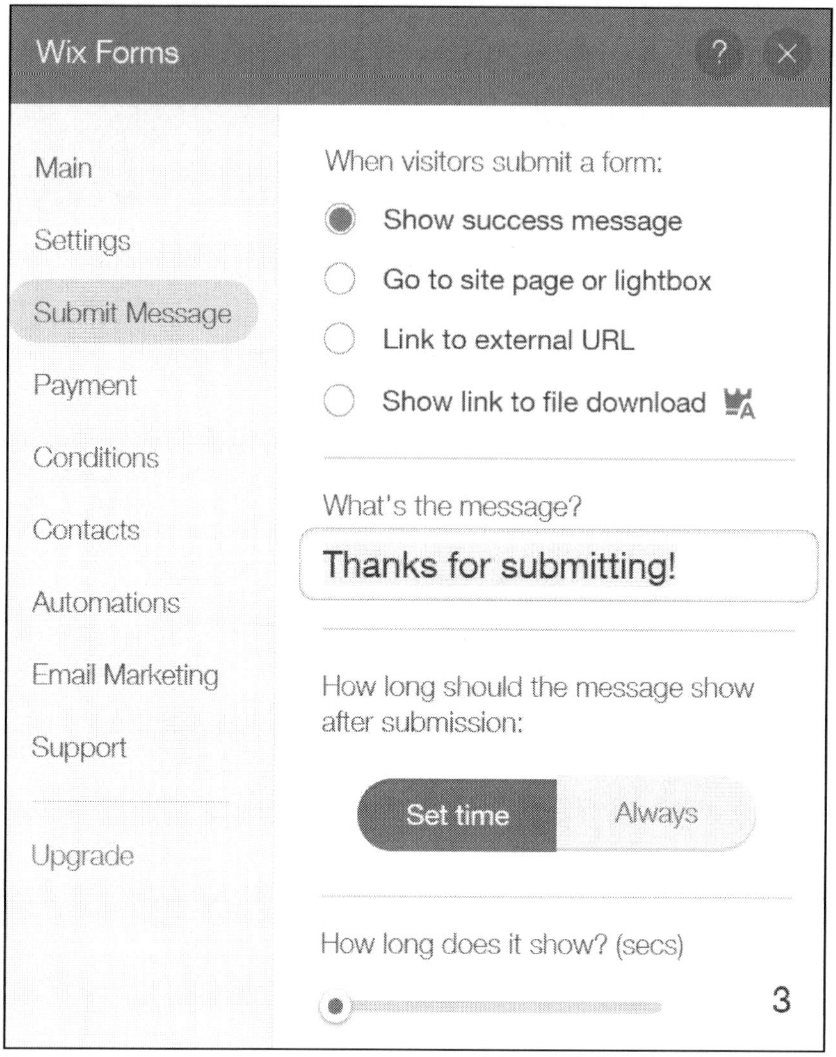

Figure 6.40

One other thing you might want to adjust is the fields within your form. You can add additional fields such as a phone number field or a reCAPTCHA option where people will have to take an additional step before submitting their question to make sure they are a real person and not a web bot sending spam to your email address via your contact form. You can add these fields by clicking on the *Add New Field* button when you click on your form in the editor.

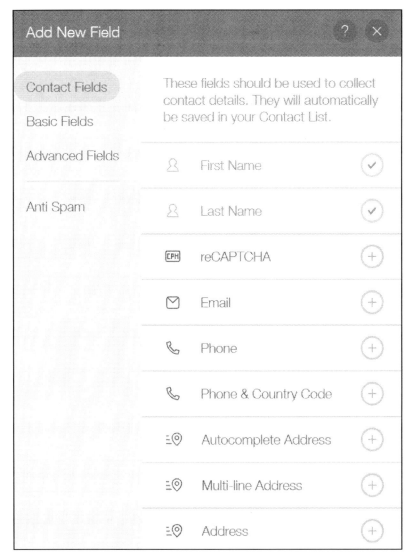

Figure 6.41

Location Maps

If you have a business with a physical address, you might want to include a map to your location on your contact page so your visitors will be able to see where you are located and find out how to get to your business.

Once again, my template came with an included map so I will create a new one from scratch rather than edit the existing one. If your template came with a map then you might just want to edit it rather than start from the beginning.

To add a map you will need to click on the Add button and go back to the *Contact & Forms* section and select the type of map you wish to add. You have two choices for the map type with one being a smaller, rectangle shaped and the other a longer, full width map.

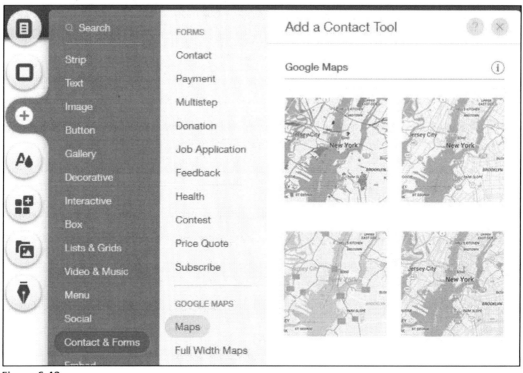

Figure 6.42

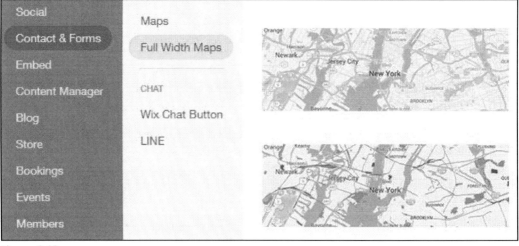

Figure 6.43

For my example, I will use the smaller option since I feel it will better suit the position on the page where I plan on placing it. Once the map is on my page I can then click on the *Manage Locations* button to configure the location of my bakery. The default location is the Wix Office address which you will want to change of course.

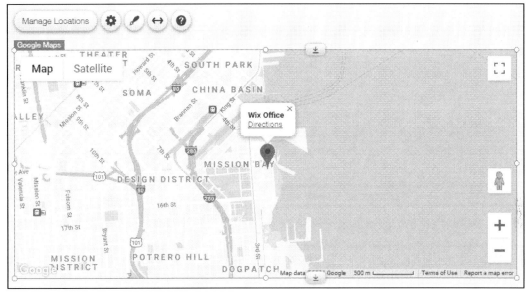

Figure 6.44

If you have more than one location, you can add each one of them to your map assuming they are not so far away that your map will be zoomed out too far for it to make sense to your visitors.

Now I will add the address of my bakery and also change the title from Wix Office to Triple C Bakery. You can also add a description of your business if desired.

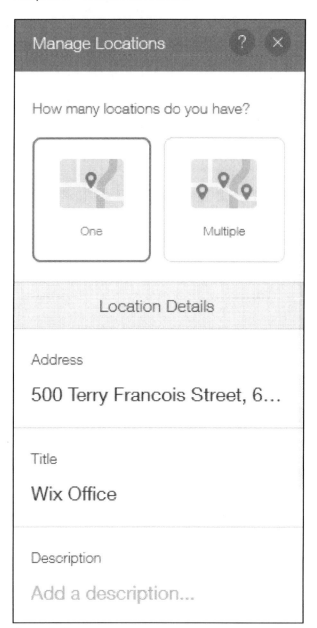

Figure 6.45

Now I have a map on my page showing the location of my bakery so my visitors can see where I am located. They can also click on the *Directions* link under the bakery name to get turn by turn directions from wherever they may be.

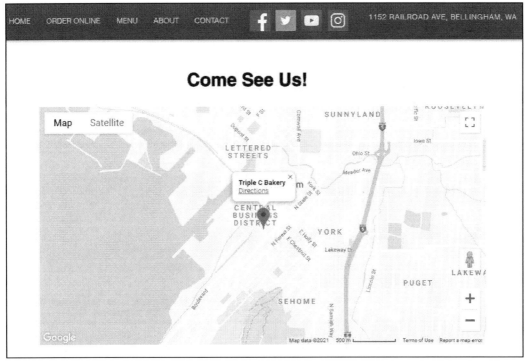

Figure 6.46

Blogs

Blogging is a great way to showcase your ideas, products or services or can just be a way for you to connect with your visitors to keep them informed about what is going on regarding the topic of your website. You can think of a blog as a diary or journal for your ideas or opinions. It can also be used to let people know about upcoming events or new products on the horizon.

To add a blog, you will once again to the *Add* menu and choose *Blog*. Then you will be prompted as to what type of blog you wish to create. You can choose a basic blog, a blog with a writing team or a member's blog where others can contribute their own content assuming they have a membership to your site.

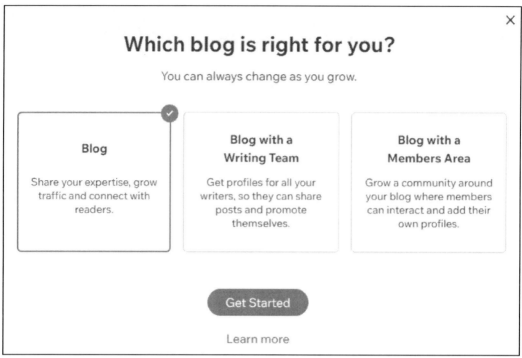

Figure 6.47

For my example, I will choose the basic blog since I will be the only one updating my site with the latest baked goods. After I clicked on the *Get Started* button, a new page named Blog was created and some sample content was added. Also when I go to my Pages section, I will see a section called *Blog Pages*.

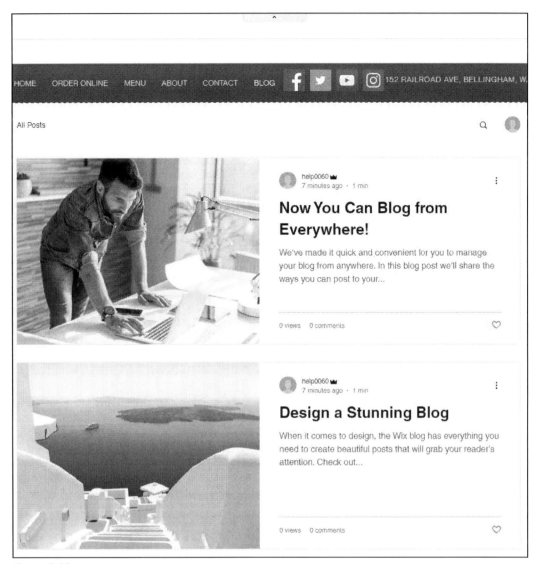

Figure 6.48

Figure 6.49

When I select the blog on my page I will get a button that says *Manage Posts*. After I click the button I will be taken to my blog section where I can then edit or remove the sample blogs that Wix created and also create a new blog by clicking on the *Create New Post* button.

Figure 6.50

Clicking on the ellipsis next to a post will give me options to edit, duplicate, delete or revert the post to draft status. I will now remove all the sample blog posts and create a new one of my own. I can do things such as add text, and images and format them the same way I can on other pages. I can even add links if needed.

Off to the left of the blog post, you will see various buttons that will allow you to change the settings for the post such as the date it was posted and the author who wrote it. You can also set up SEO settings for search engines like you can with your main site and add tags that are related to the blog content which is also used for search engines so they can find your posts. You can even create multiple categories for your blog posts to help keep things organized.

Once I have everything looking the way I like I can click on the *Publish* button. If I click the down arrow next to the Publish button I can save my post as a draft or schedule it to go live at a certain time.

Figure 6.51

Now when I go back to my blog page I will see my new post with its posting date and can then see how my people have viewed it, liked it and I can also read any comments that might have been made about it.

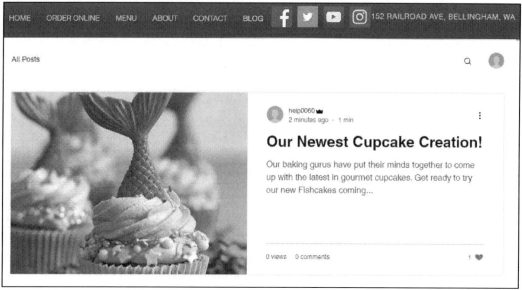

Figure 6.52

Wix Logo Maker Website

If you don't have a logo for your website and wish to create one then you can either do it yourself using some design software or create one using the Wix Logo Maker website.

When you get to the website (**https://www.wix.com/logo/maker**) you will click the *Start Now* button and then you will be asked if you want to hire a professional designer or create the logo yourself. So if you don't have any artistic skills you might want to pay someone to create it for you or you can always try it yourself first.

If you decide to create your own logo then you will be asked to enter your company name and an optional tagline.

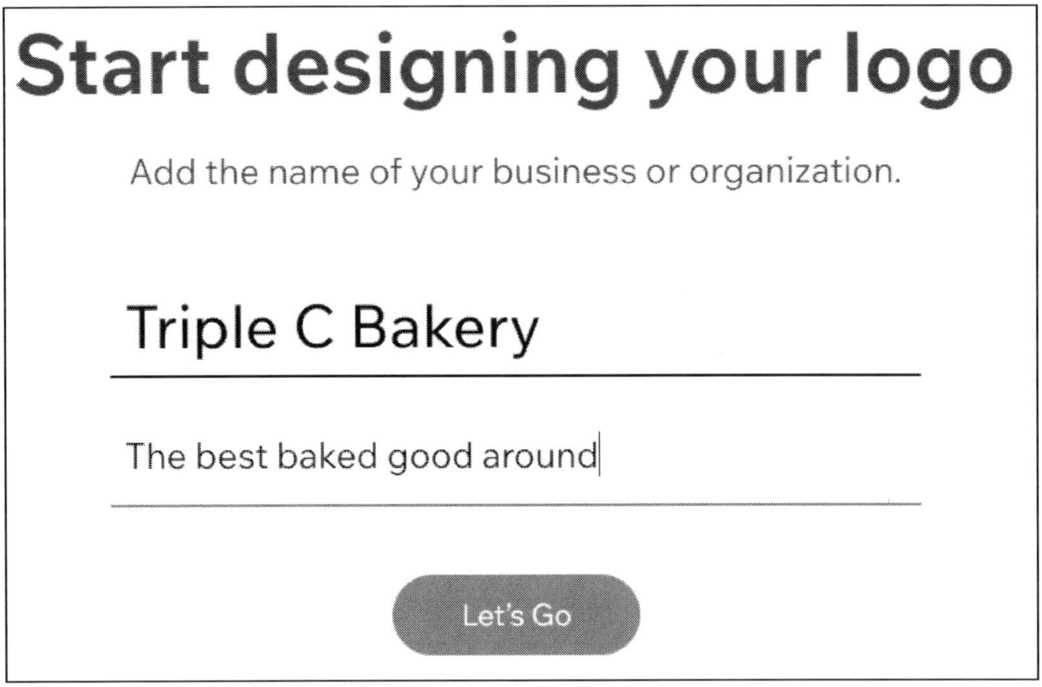

Start designing your logo

Add the name of your business or organization.

Triple C Bakery

The best baked good around|

Let's Go

Figure 6.53

Then you can type in the type of business that applies to your website and the logo maker will give you some choices to select from based on what you type in this area. So when I type in bakery, the closest thing that comes up is wholesale bakery.

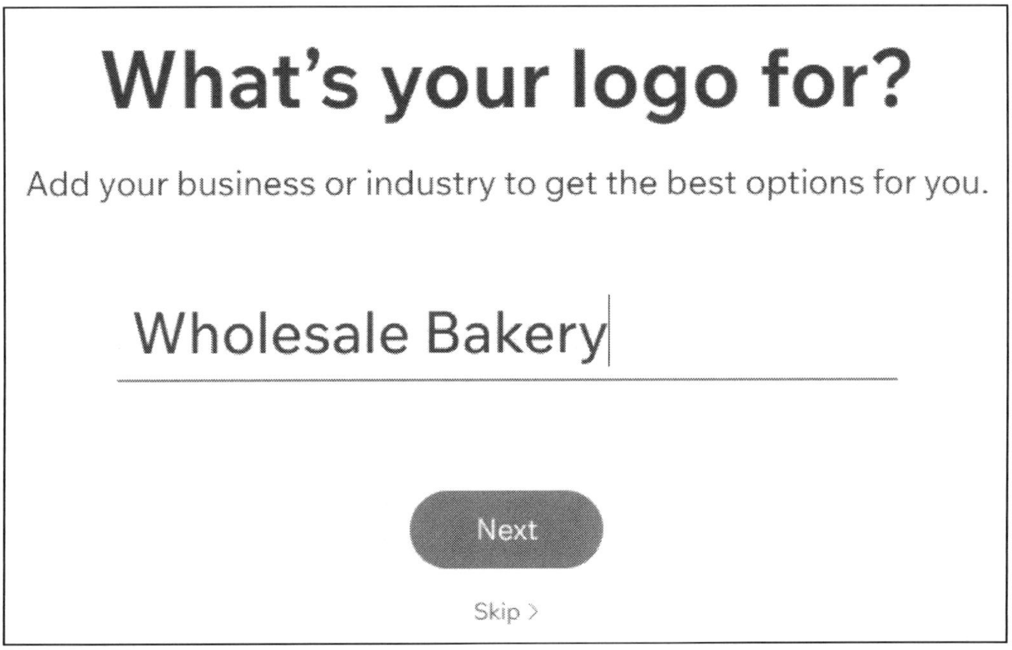

What's your logo for?

Add your business or industry to get the best options for you.

Wholesale Bakery|

Next

Skip >

Figure 6.54

Next, you can choose a design type for your logo. I will click on *Fresh* and then the *Next* button.

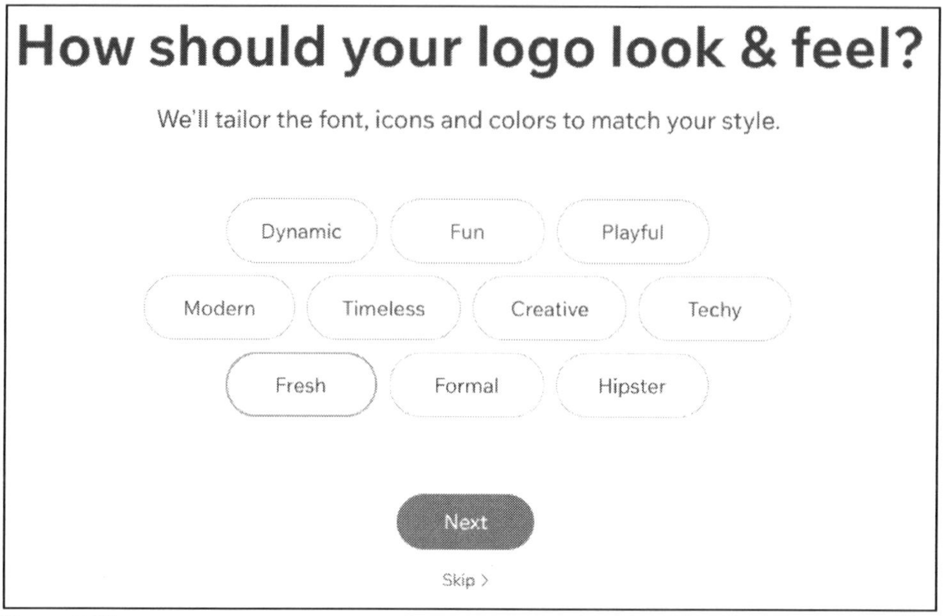

Figure 6.55

Next, you will be shown some sample logos and you can choose one of these or click on *I don't like either of them* to be shown some additional options. When you click on a sample you will be shown additional samples so the logo maker can get a few ideas of what you like.

Figure 6.56

Next, you will be asked where you plan to use this logo.

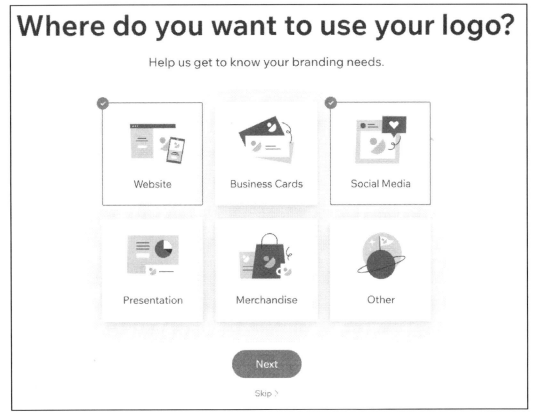

Figure 6.57

Now I will need to choose one of the many sample logos that I can then customize to fit what I had in mind for my design.

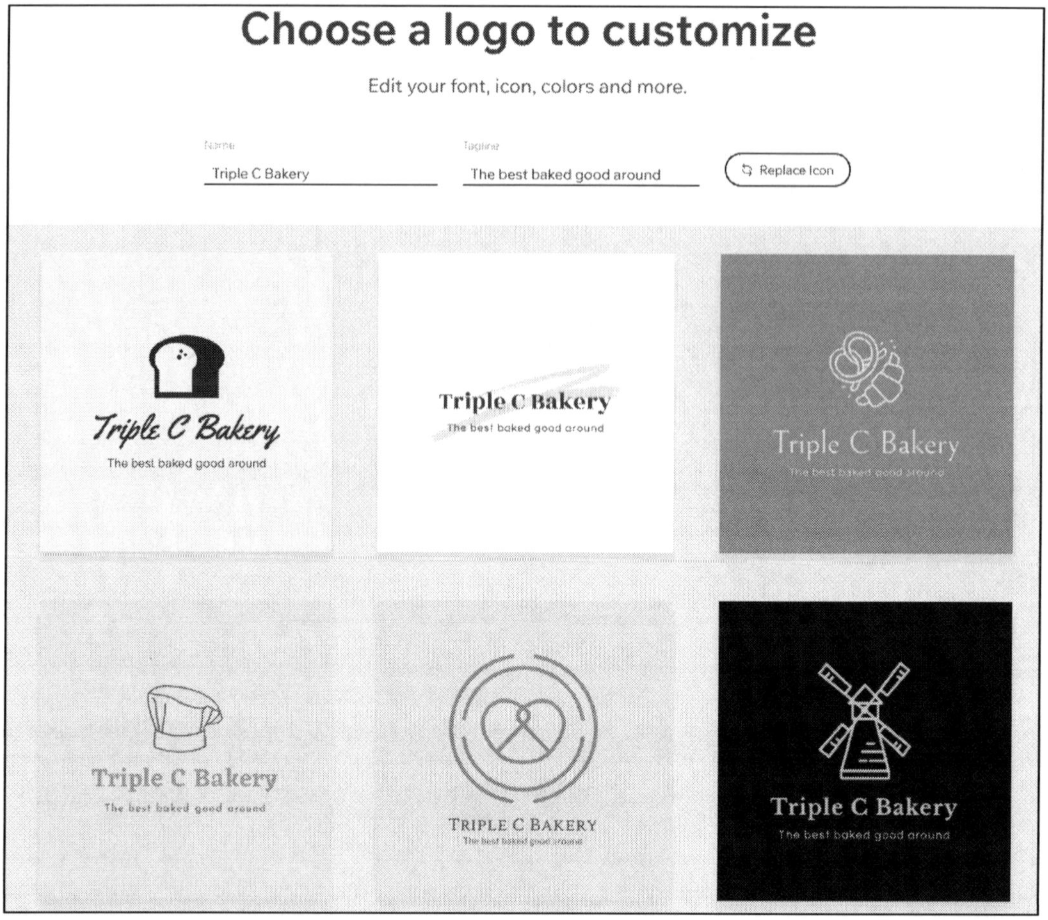

Figure 6.58

Now I can edit my design by changing its colors, fonts, icons, backgrounds and so on. I can even add shapes such as a circle around my design to make it stand out. After everything looks good I will click on the *Next* button.

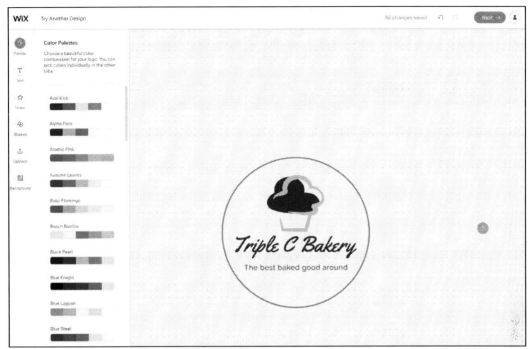

Figure 6.59

I can then choose to purchase my logo and will have a couple of options as to what features I wish to buy such as social media logo files for an additional cost. Then after I purchase my logo I can then download it and then upload it to my Media Manager to use on my website.

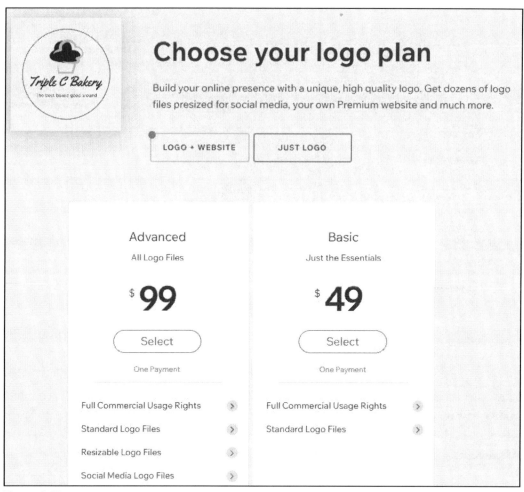

Figure 6.60

SEO (Search Engine Optimization)

One of the main reasons for putting your ideas, products or services on a website is so that other people can see what you have to say or spend their money on the products or services you provide. So if nobody can find you, there is no real reason to create a website.

Sure you might be creating a website for something such as your softball team so you can post pictures and videos and maybe some announcements. If this is the case then you will most likely be sharing your website's URL (address) and people will be able to access your site that way.

But if your goal is to reach people you don't know then your site will need to be indexed in search engines so when someone searches for a term related to the content of your website, yours will show up. Getting yourself found is not as easy as you might think though. If your website is about a common topic or product then you will have a lot of competition when it comes to being found in web searches. In fact, there are companies out there that specialize in getting your website found by others when they search for sites similar to yours. These services come at a cost and often involve a monthly fee for maintenance, and they can be pricey as well.

Wix offers some tools that will help to get your website found with Google which is the #1 search engine if you didn't already know that. These tools won't replace these SEO services, but they can help get you pointed in the right direction and are definitely better than not doing anything at all.

To get to the SEO settings you can click on the Settings menu and then choose *Get Found on Google*.

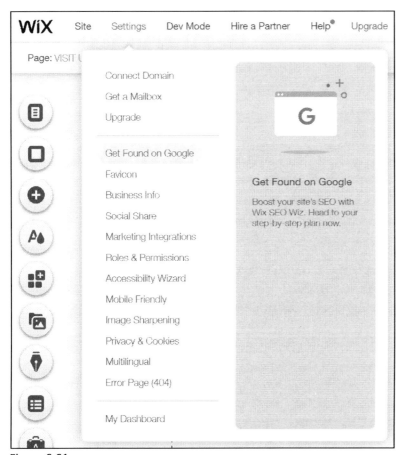

Figure 6.61

From there you can click on SEO tools on the left hand side to see all of your SEO options.

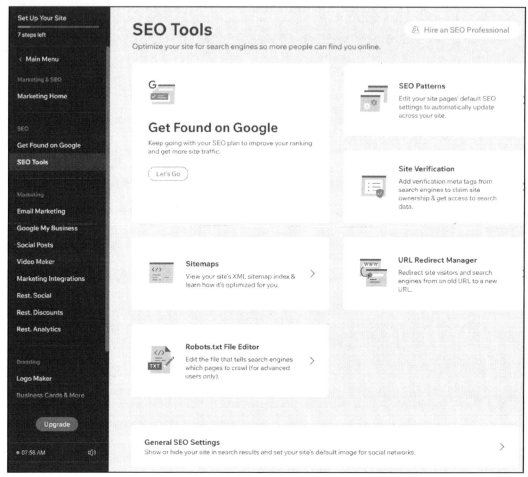

Figure 6.62

One of the first things you want to do is go to *General SEO Settings* and enable the setting for *Let search engines index your site* and then add your site image for the *general social image* section if you have one.

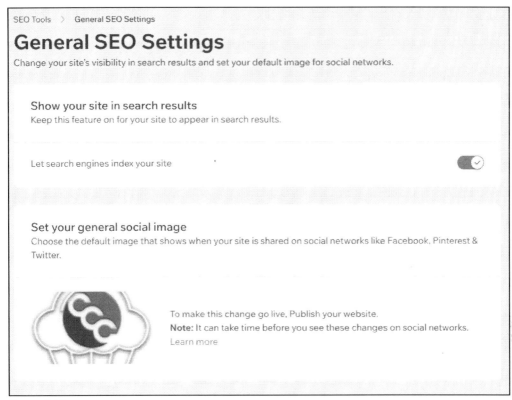

SEO Tools > General SEO Settings

General SEO Settings

Change your site's visibility in search results and set your default image for social networks.

Show your site in search results

Keep this feature on for your site to appear in search results.

Let search engines index your site

Set your general social image

Choose the default image that shows when your site is shared on social networks like Facebook, Pinterest & Twitter.

To make this change go live, Publish your website.

Note: It can take time before you see these changes on social networks.

Learn more

Figure 6.63

Then I would go back to the SEO tools and click on *Get Found on Google* to start the Wix SEO Wizard.

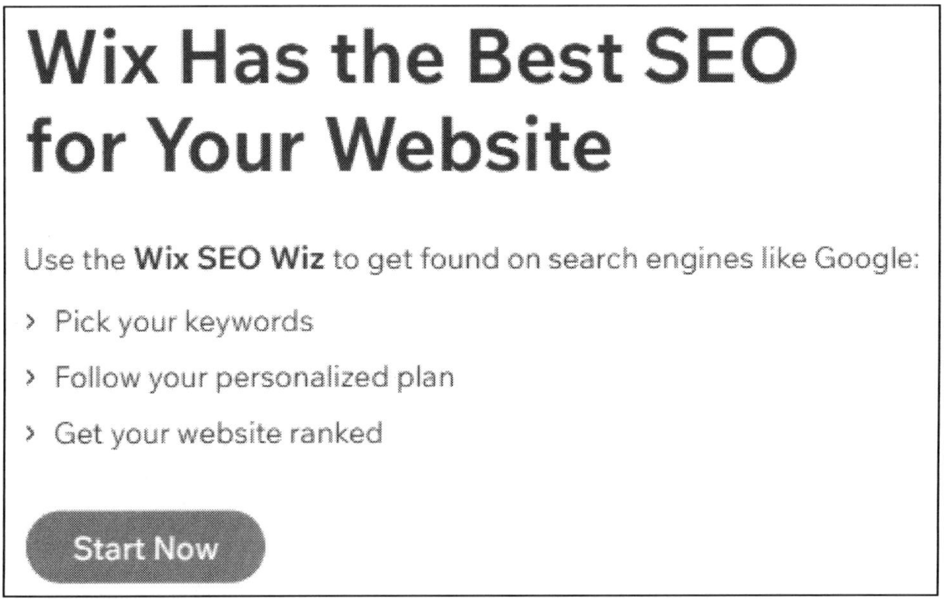

Wix Has the Best SEO for Your Website

Use the **Wix SEO Wiz** to get found on search engines like Google:

> Pick your keywords

> Follow your personalized plan

> Get your website ranked

Start Now

Figure 6.64

Next, you will enter your website name. Your website name and business name should be the same for the best results.

Figure 6.65

If your business has an address, you can enter it in this next step. I will add my made up address since my bakery doesn't really exist.

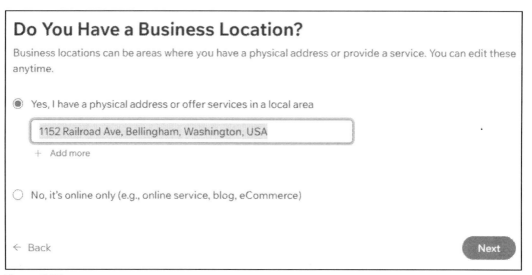

Figure 6.66

Now I will need to add some keyword phrases that describe my bakery. You only get three so make sure you use the best wording you can. You can have more than one word per phrase so try not to only use one word keywords. Once I have my keywords in place I will then click the *Create SEO Plan button* to be brought to my custom SEO plan (figure 6.68).

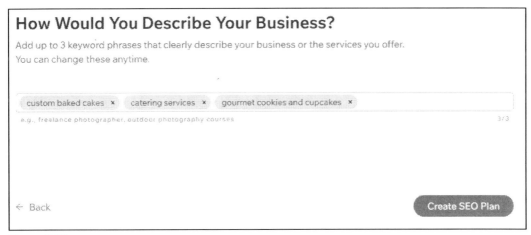

Figure 6.67

The plan is then broken down into three steps that you will need to complete as best you can. Your results will most likely look different than mine depending on your site configuration.

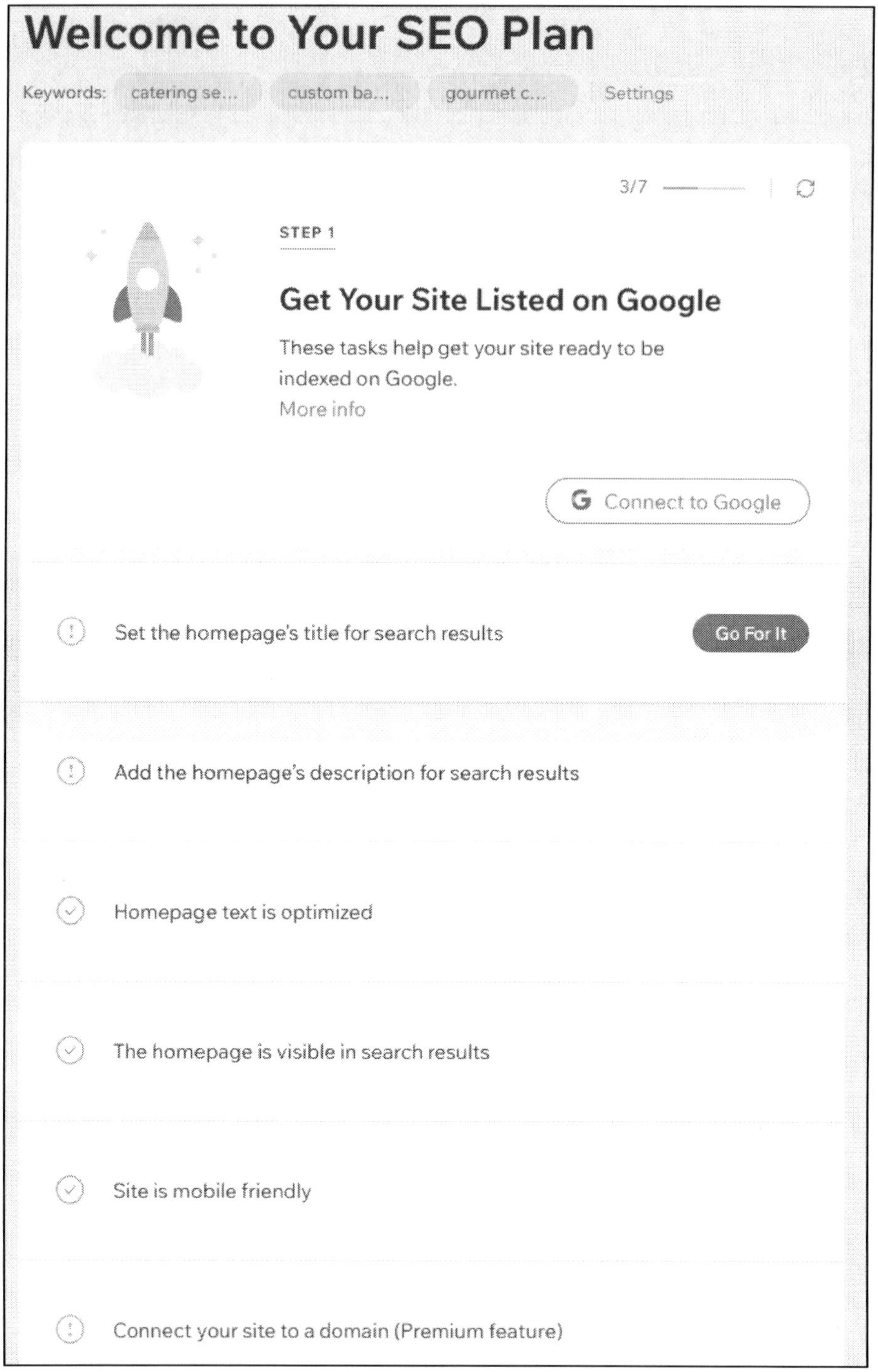

Welcome to Your SEO Plan

Keywords: catering se...   custom ba...   gourmet c...   Settings

3/7 ———— | ⟳

STEP 1

Get Your Site Listed on Google

These tasks help get your site ready to be
indexed on Google.

More info

G Connect to Google

(!) Set the homepage's title for search results   **Go For It**

(!) Add the homepage's description for search results

(✓) Homepage text is optimized

(✓) The homepage is visible in search results

(✓) Site is mobile friendly

(!) Connect your site to a domain (Premium feature)

Figure 6.68

Then you will need to go through all of the items that are marked with a red
exclamation point to complete your SEO setup. For example, if I click on the first

one that says Set the homepage's title for search results I will be brought to an area with instructions on how to complete this step.

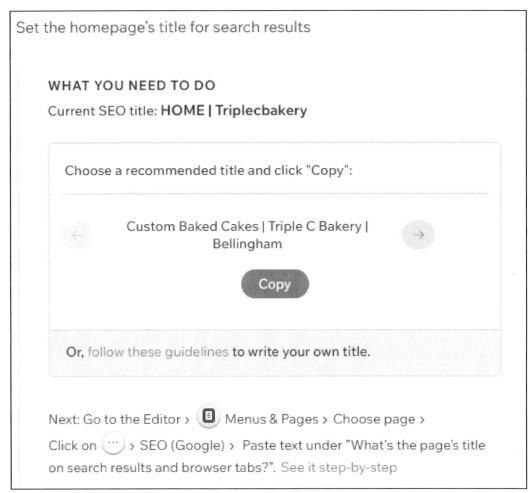

Figure 6.69

After I complete all of the sections for Step 1, I can then move to Step 2 which has similar tasks. After that, I can go to Step 3 which is more of an informational step.

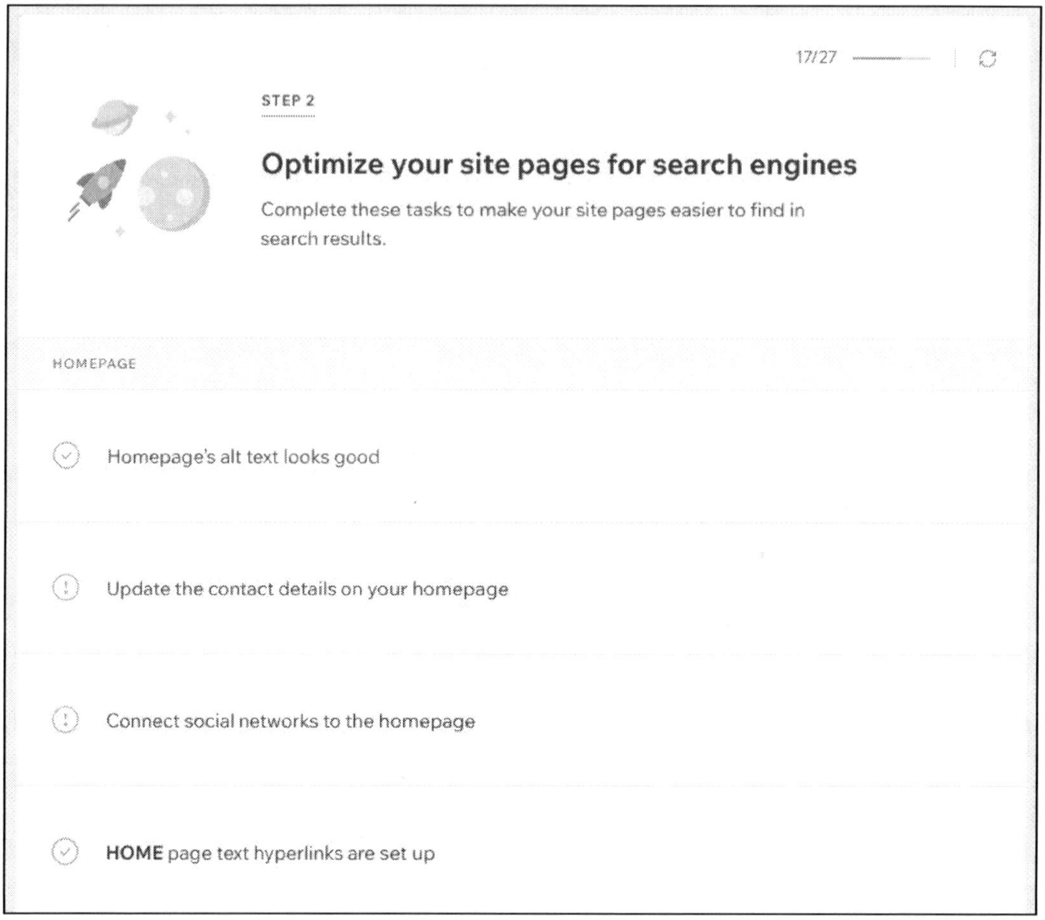
17/27
STEP 2
Optimize your site pages for search engines
Complete these tasks to make your site pages easier to find in search results.
HOMEPAGE
Homepage's alt text looks good
Update the contact details on your homepage
Connect social networks to the homepage
HOME page text hyperlinks are set up
Figure 6.70

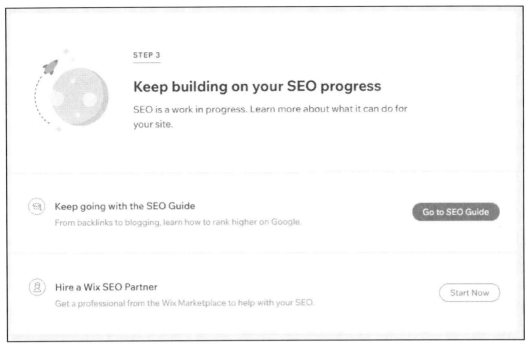

STEP 3

Keep building on your SEO progress

SEO is a work in progress. Learn more about what it can do for your site.

Keep going with the SEO Guide

From backlinks to blogging, learn how to rank higher on Google.

Go to SEO Guide

Hire a Wix SEO Partner

Get a professional from the Wix Marketplace to help with your SEO.

Start Now

Figure 6.71

You can also perform SEO tasks on a page by page basis by going to your Main Pages section and then to the SEO (Google) tab. Here you can change the Google preview as well as the page URL and its title. Then if you like you can add a description of the page contents to help for search purposes. If you would like a particular page to be hidden from searches you can disable that feature from here as well.

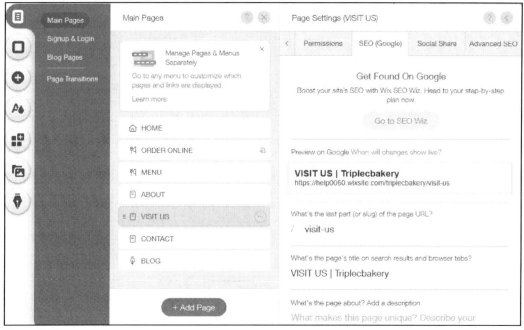

Figure 6.72

Site Search Box

If your website is on the larger side and contains many pages and a lot of information then you might want to add a search box to your site. This is different from a Google search and is just a way for your visitors to search the contents of your website while actually on your website.

To add a search box you will need to go to the *Add* button and then choose *Store* and then *Wix Search Site*.

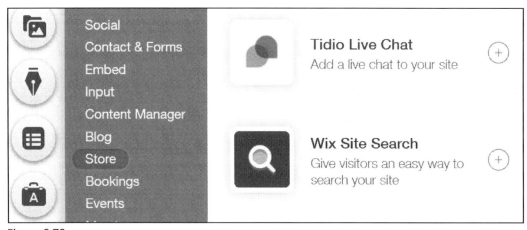

Figure 6.73

Then you can drag your search box anywhere you like on the page and you might want to place it in the header or footer so it will show up on every page of your site (of you have room). I placed my search box in the header to the left of my business address.

Figure 6.74

Once you add a search box you will see that you have a new page on your site called *Search Results*.

Figure 6.75

If you don't like how this search box works then you can search for a search box app and try out another option. I will be discussing apps in the next section. If you need to test out the search feature then you will need to publish your website first. I will be discussing publishing options in Chapter 8.

Installing Apps

One of the great things about using Wix to create your website is that you are not limited to using only the features that are provided with Wix itself. While creating your website, you might want to add a component that is not available with Wix. If that is the case, then you can search for an app that is designed to add the functionality you are looking for to your site.

To see the available apps or search for an app you can click on the *Add Apps* button in the Wix editor, and you will be shown some recommended apps as well as some categories that you can browse to find the app you need. You can also use the search box at the top of the page to see if you can find your app that way.

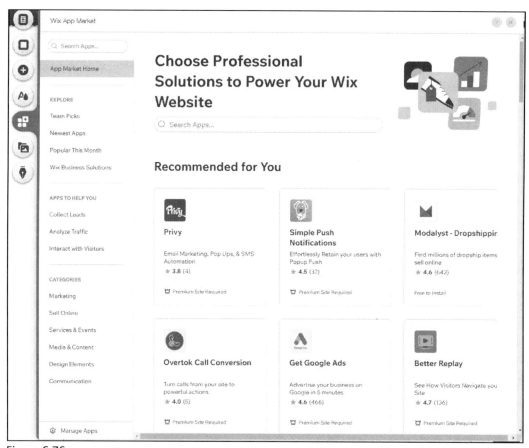

Figure 6.76

For example, if I search a different search bar for my site I will be shown what apps come up when I type in the term **search bar**. As you can see in figure 6.77, it shows the Wix Search Site app I already have installed plus another one named *Site Search*. It also shows their user ratings which you can then click on to read if you like. You will also notice that it found some apps that are not related to my search, at least as far as I am concerned.

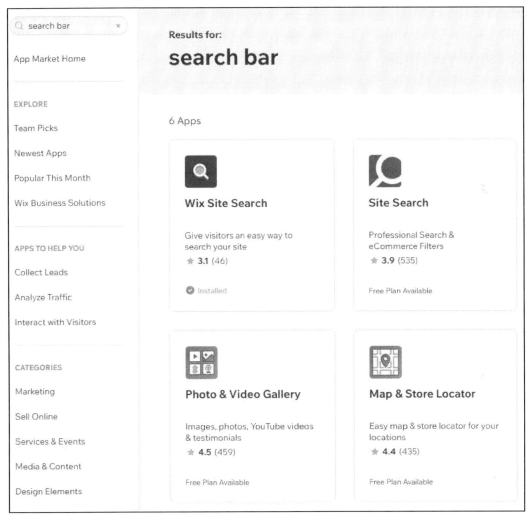

Figure 6.77

One thing to watch for is to make sure that any app you install is free unless you don't mind paying for a premium plan. Some will also have free trials and others will have a free version and a premium version with more features. You can see if an app is free or not at the bottom of each one.

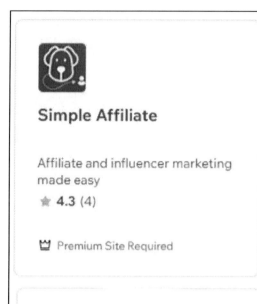

Simple Affiliate

Affiliate and influencer marketing
made easy
⭐ 4.3 (4)

👑 Premium Site Required

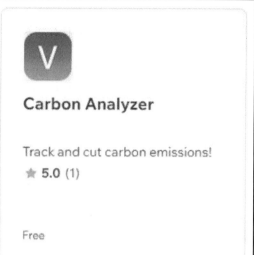

Carbon Analyzer

Track and cut carbon emissions!
⭐ 5.0 (1)

Free

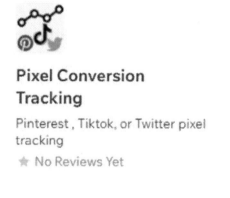

Pixel Conversion Tracking

Pinterest , Tiktok, or Twitter pixel
tracking
⭐ No Reviews Yet

7 Day Free Trial

FB & Google Ads by ROI Hunter

Automate your advertising on
Facebook & Google
⭐ No Reviews Yet

Free Plan Available

Figure 6.78

I am going to install an app called *Comments* that allows visitors to make comments on my site. When you click on the app you will be able to read a description of the app, see screenshots or a video, as well as read reviews.

If the app looks like something you want to try out you can click on the *Add to Site* button to install it on your website.

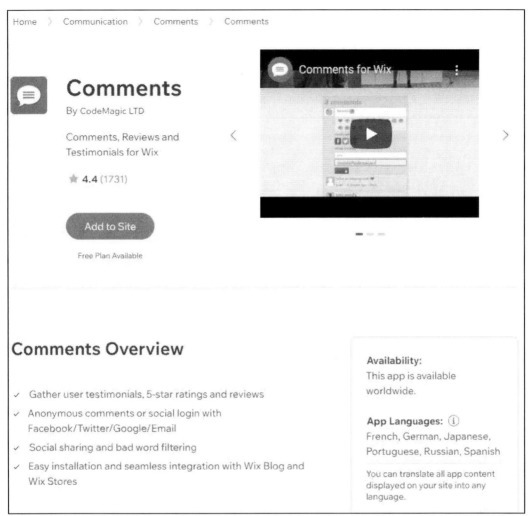

Figure 6.79

You will then be shown what site permissions the app requires to function on your website. If everything looks good then you can click on the *Add to Site* button again.

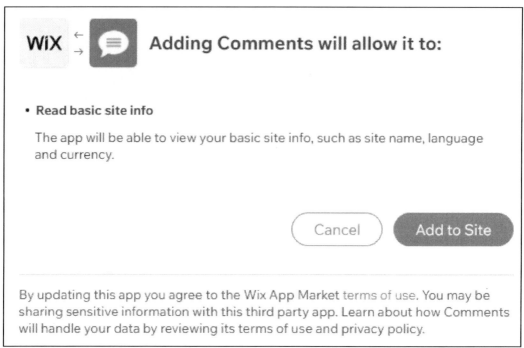

Figure 6.80

You will then most likely need to perform some type of configuration with the app to get it to work properly on your site.

Figure 6.81

Now when people go to my site they can post a comment on whichever page I have the comment box located on.

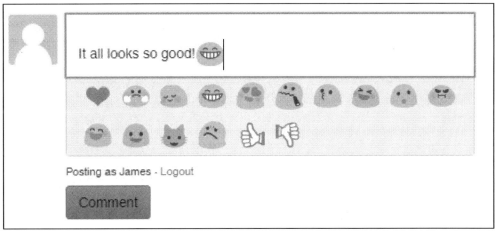

Figure 6.82

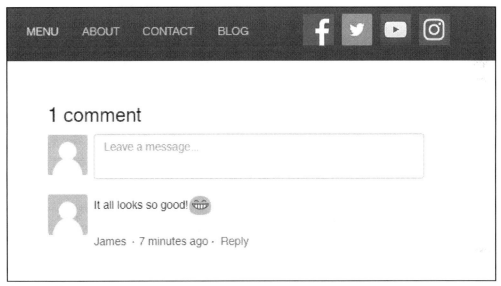

Figure 6.83

 When you add an object like a picture, search box, text box etc. to a page, it will usually just be shown on the page where you created it unless you put it in the header or footer. If you want to duplicate an object you can simply right click on it and choose Copy and then paste it on to a different page.

Chapter 7 - Tools and Settings

There are many (almost too many) settings and configuration options available to you when you create a website using Wix. Granted, many of them you will never need to use but you should still know how to find a particular setting if you ever need to make changes.

The Wix settings are not all in one place, but you should still be able to find what you are looking for if you search around enough. I'm sure you have seen the Settings menu item at the top of the dashboard, and I have mentioned it a few times already. This Settings menu only has a fraction of the available settings and tools you can use to configure your website.

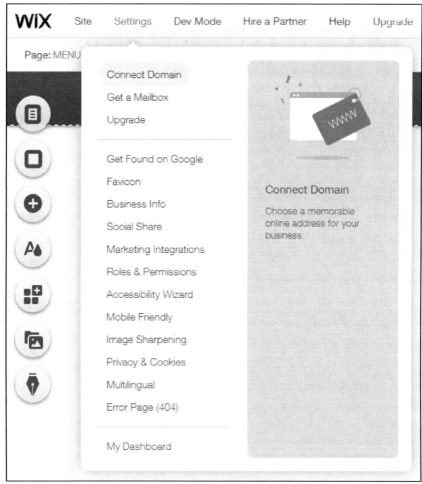

Figure 7.1

Wix Dashboard

If you are looking for the place where you can find most of the settings and configuration options for your site then you will need to open the Wix Dashboard which can be found by clicking on *My Dashboard* at the bottom of the settings menu as seen in figure 7.1.

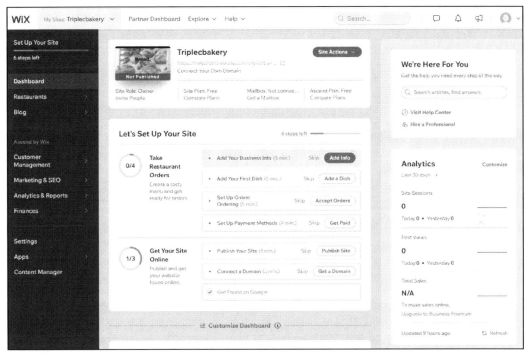

Figure 7.2

Depending on the type of template you used (if any) and what other features you have on your website will determine how your dashboard looks. Since I used a bakery template, I have options to set up restaurant orders which you might not have in your dashboard.

To the right of the main window you will see your *Analytics* section which will give you information about things like website traffic, blog posts and sales. You won't see much here until after your site is published. Figure 7.3 shows the *Suggested For You* section that contains recommendations for other items you can add to your website such as getting an email address or connecting your site to Google.

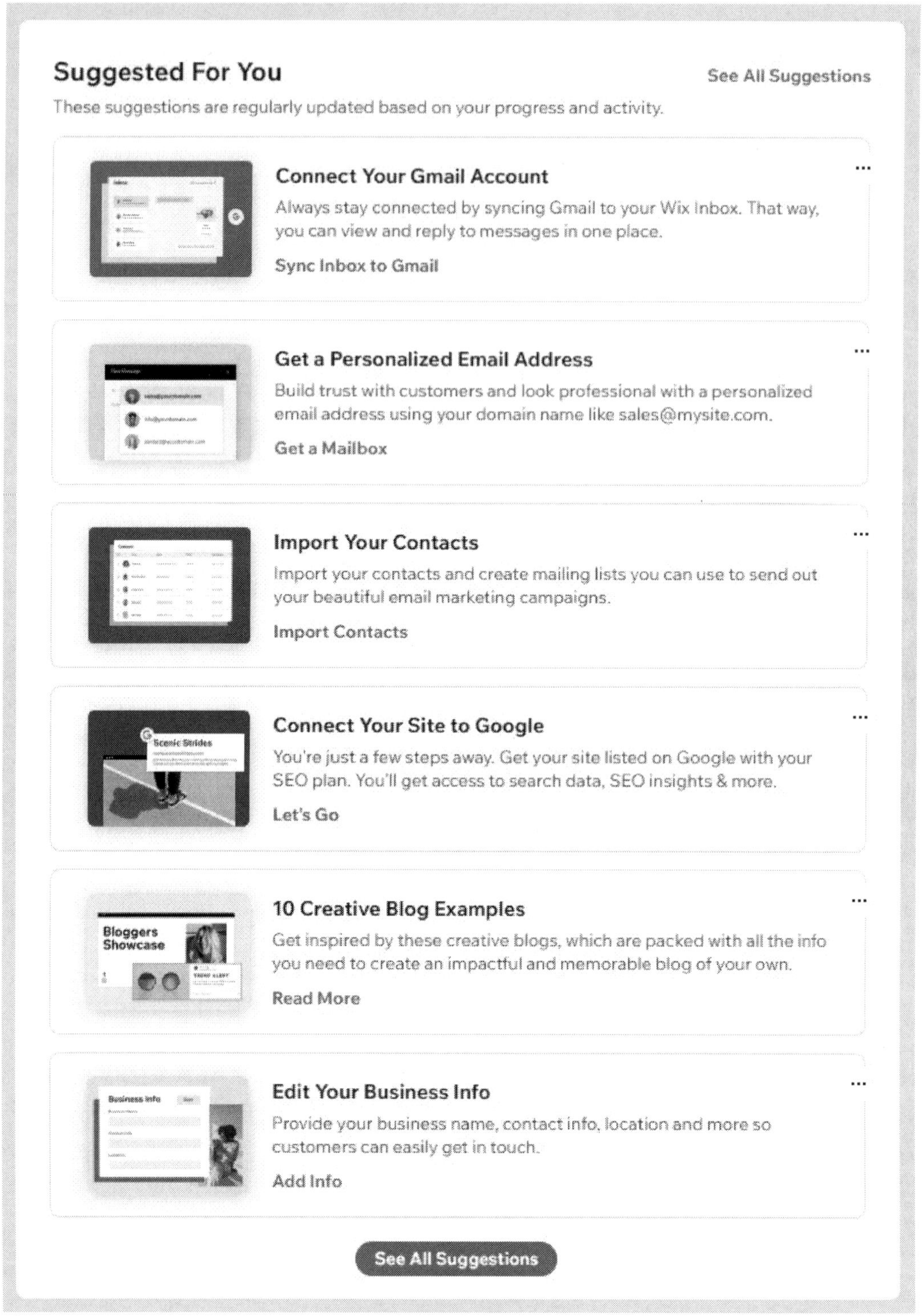
Suggested For You
See All Suggestions
These suggestions are regularly updated based on your progress and activity.
Connect Your Gmail Account
Always stay connected by syncing Gmail to your Wix Inbox. That way, you can view and reply to messages in one place.
Sync Inbox to Gmail
Get a Personalized Email Address
Build trust with customers and look professional with a personalized email address using your domain name like sales@mysite.com.
Get a Mailbox
Import Your Contacts
Import your contacts and create mailing lists you can use to send out your beautiful email marketing campaigns.
Import Contacts
Connect Your Site to Google
Scenic Strides
You're just a few steps away. Get your site listed on Google with your SEO plan. You'll get access to search data, SEO insights & more.
Let's Go
10 Creative Blog Examples
Bloggers Showcase
Get inspired by these creative blogs, which are packed with all the info you need to create an impactful and memorable blog of your own.
Read More
Edit Your Business Info
Business Info
Provide your business name, contact info, location and more so customers can easily get in touch.
Add Info
See All Suggestions
Figure 7.3

Figure 7.4 shows you even more tools and features that you can add to your site as well as a way to check settings and reports. I would click through these items to see if any of them might be something you want to implement on your site.

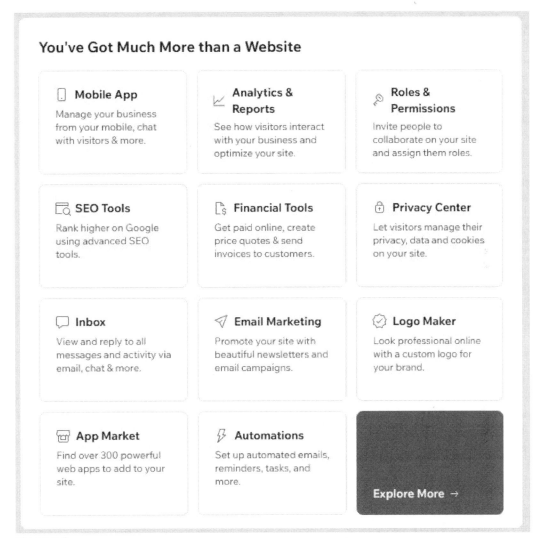

Figure 7.4

There is also a section called *Marketing & SEO* that you can click on to bring up a submenu with a variety of tasks you can perform to help improve your website's visibility and performance.

Figure 7.5

Once your site is complete and has been live for a period of time, you can come back to the *Analytics & Reports* section to get information about site visits, sales (if you have that setup), traffic sources and website performance. You can also view reports on your site behavior as well.

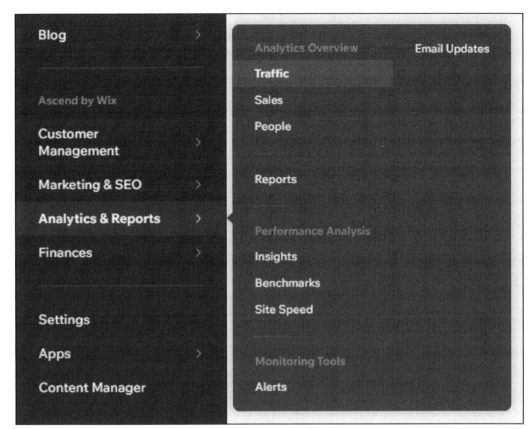

Figure 7.6

Clicking on *Settings* will bring you to another section (figure 7.7) with even more settings than you will want to know about! Clicking the arrow next to each setting will take you to a new page where you can then make changes to that particular setting. I know this is a bit overwhelming but keep in mind that you will most likely never use many of these settings and if your site is working the way you want it to, you shouldn't have to worry about them. It's a good idea to poke around here just to get an idea of the things you can configure if needed.

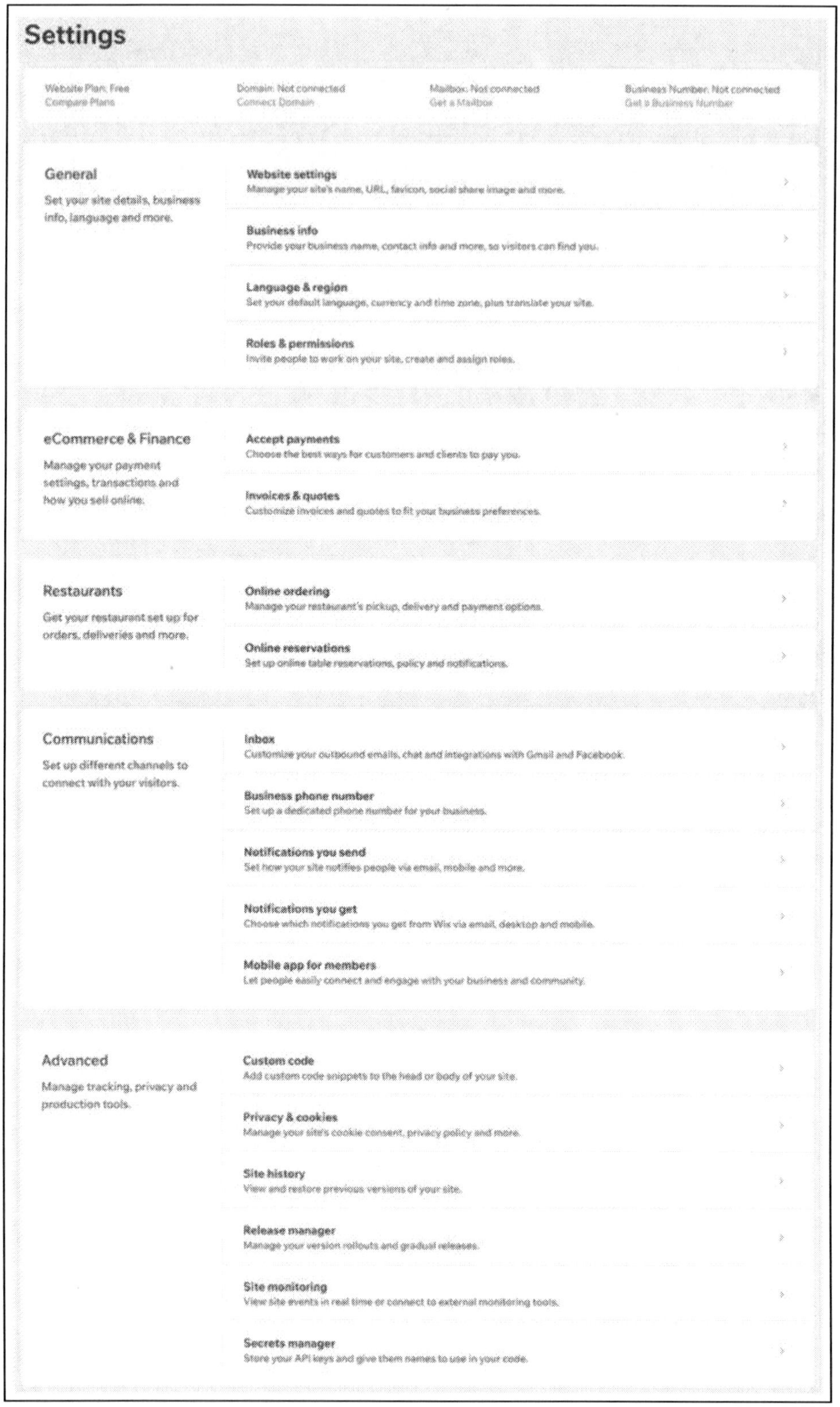

Settings

| Website Plan: Free | Domain: Not connected | Mailbox: Not connected | Business Number: Not connected |
| Compare Plans | Connect Domain | Get a Mailbox | Get a Business Number |

General
Set your site details, business info, language and more.

Website settings
Manage your site's name, URL, favicon, social share image and more. >

Business info
Provide your business name, contact info and more, so visitors can find you. >

Language & region
Set your default language, currency and time zone, plus translate your site. >

Roles & permissions
Invite people to work on your site, create and assign roles. >

eCommerce & Finance
Manage your payment settings, transactions and how you sell online.

Accept payments
Choose the best ways for customers and clients to pay you. >

Invoices & quotes
Customize invoices and quotes to fit your business preferences. >

Restaurants
Get your restaurant set up for orders, deliveries and more.

Online ordering
Manage your restaurant's pickup, delivery and payment options. >

Online reservations
Set up online table reservations, policy and notifications. >

Communications
Set up different channels to connect with your visitors.

Inbox
Customize your outbound emails, chat and integrations with Gmail and Facebook. >

Business phone number
Set up a dedicated phone number for your business. >

Notifications you send
Set how your site notifies people via email, mobile and more. >

Notifications you get
Choose which notifications you get from Wix via email, desktop and mobile. >

Mobile app for members
Let people easily connect and engage with your business and community. >

Advanced
Manage tracking, privacy and production tools.

Custom code
Add custom code snippets to the head or body of your site. >

Privacy & cookies
Manage your site's cookie consent, privacy policy and more. >

Site history
View and restore previous versions of your site. >

Release manager
Manage your version rollouts and gradual releases. >

Site monitoring
View site events in real time or connect to external monitoring tools. >

Secrets manager
Store your API keys and give them names to use in your code. >

Figure 7.7

If you plan on using a lot of apps with your website, you might want to make a note of the *Apps* section because this is the place you can go to see what apps you have installed as well as upgrade them when there is an update. You can also remove apps by clicking the ellipsis next to the *Open* button.

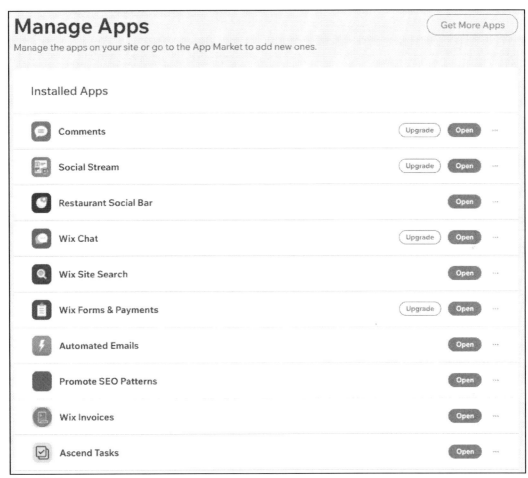

Figure 7.8

Content Manager
The Wix Content Manager is an additional feature that you can add to your dashboard for free to help manage all of the content related to your various website components such as blogs, contact forms, subscribers and so on. It is similar to the Media Manager but actually separates your content into its own sections.

To add the Content Manager to your site click on the *Add* button and then choose *Content Manager* and finally click on the *Add to Site* button.

Figure 7.9

You will then be asked to add a preset to your site which is a way to organize your content based on what you are using your site for. You can choose the *My items* selection to create your own template but I decided to be nice and share my recipes with my visitors so I will click on *Recipes* and then the *Add to Site* button.

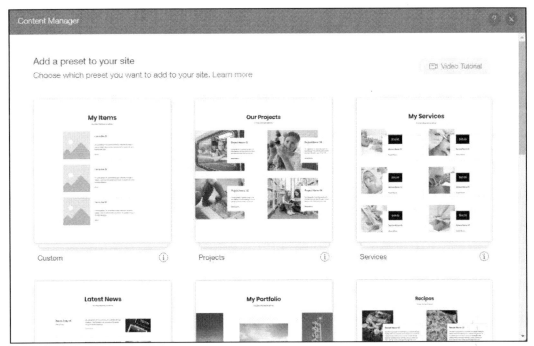

Figure 7.10

After you add the Content Manager feature to your site you will have a *Content Manager* button along with all of your other tools in the editor.

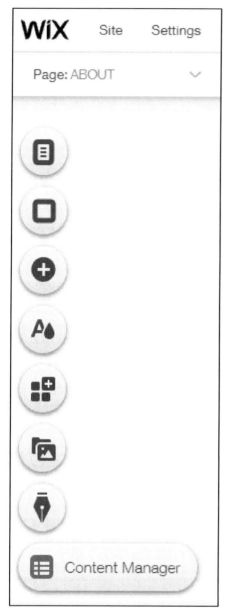

Figure 7.11

When you click this button you will see all of the content for the various components of your site. You can then click on them to manage their related content. Some of the components won't really have any content to manage so keep that in mind when you click through them.

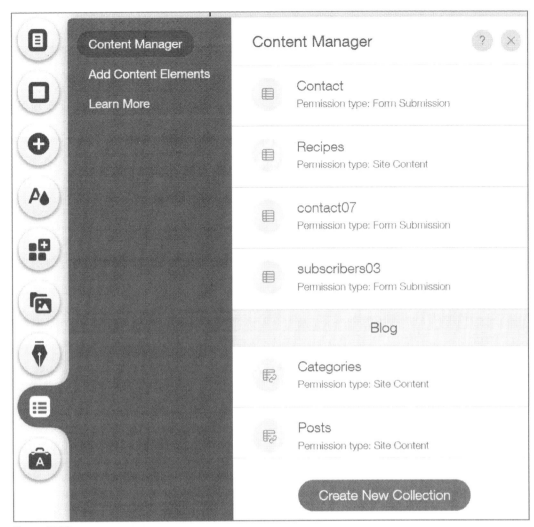

Figure 7.12

When I go to my Recipes collection I will have some preconfigured examples that I can then edit to suit my website (figures 7.13 and 7.14).

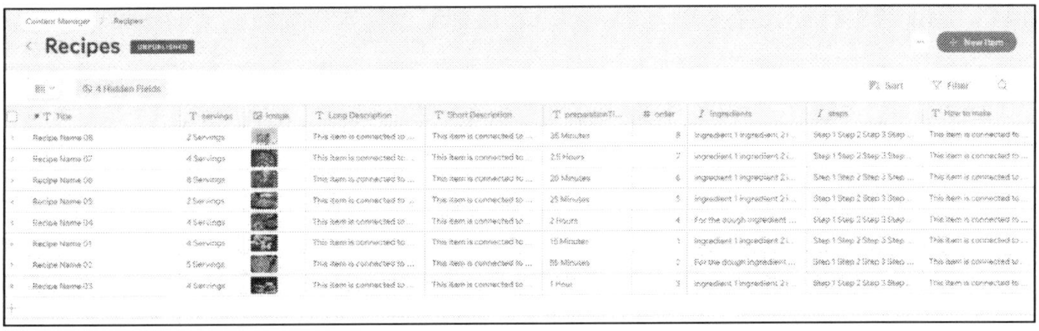

Figure 7.13

179

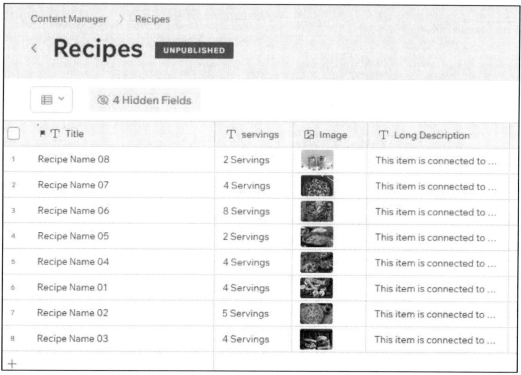

Figure 7.14

I can also decide which of the preconfigured field types I want to have shown for this collection.

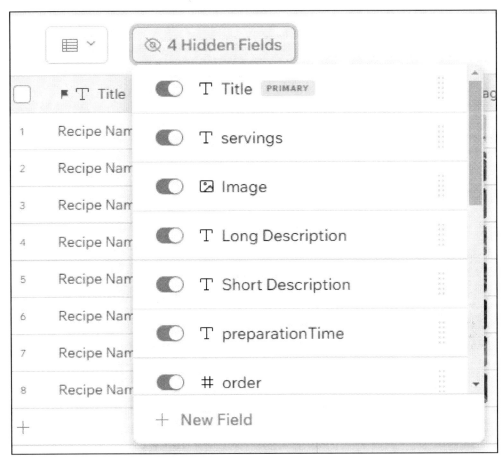

Figure 7.15

I can also change the view from a table view to a gallery view making it easier to see what I have to work with.

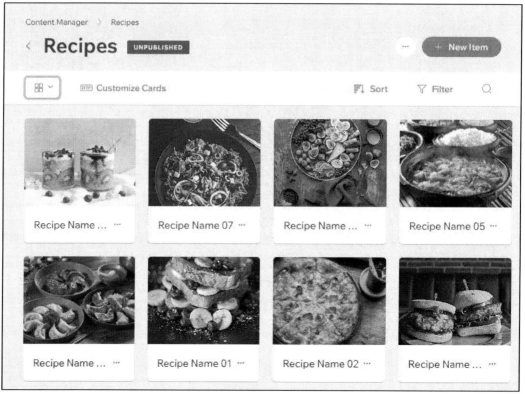

Figure 7.16

Now I will edit the names and images that came with the collection to add my own. I will leave the default sample text as is for now.

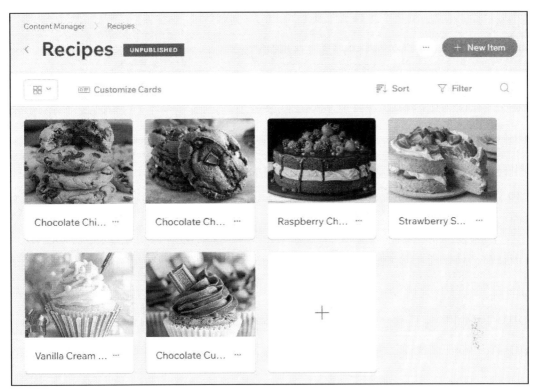

Figure 7.17

If I click on a particular item I will then be shown all of the information that goes along with that item. This information will match what was shown in the columns in figure 7.13.

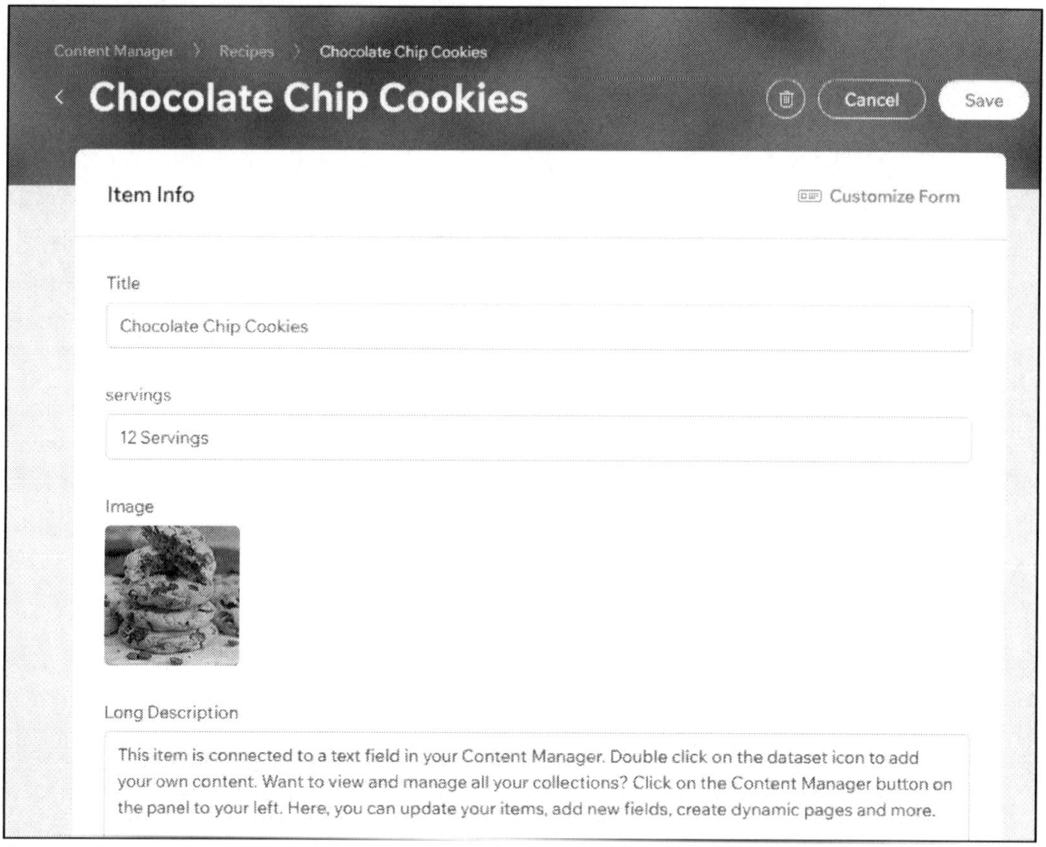

Figure 7.18

Another thing you will notice is that you will have a new page automatically created for your collection. For my template, I have a Recipes (All) and Recipes (Title) page that will display my content differently.

Figure 7.19

When I go to view that page I will see my changes and can then edit the content further to customize it to my site. I will also have a new item in my navigation\menu bar for Recipes.

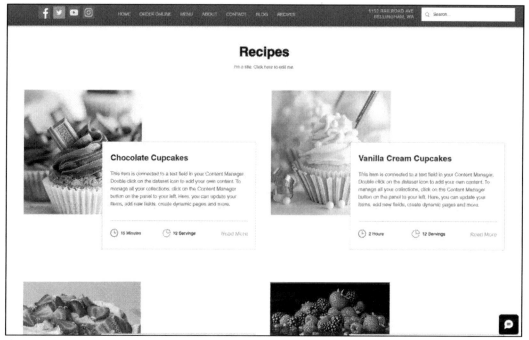

Figure 7.20

Roles and Permissions

If you are planning on having others contribute to your website so you don't need to do all of the work yourself, then you can allow other users access to your site and then assign them the roles and permissions required for them to do the work they need to do.

To configure these settings for your users you can go to the Settings menu at the top of the page and click on *Roles and Permissions*. This will then take you to your Wix Dashboard where you can view and manage these settings. As you can see in figure 7.21, I only have one user account associated with my site, and it the role of owner assigned to it.

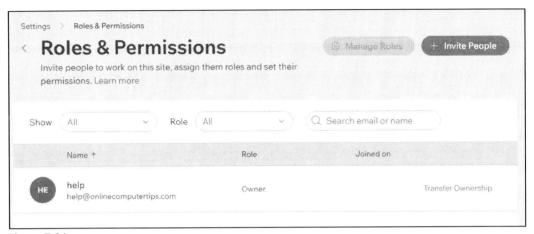

Figure 7.21

If I want to allow someone else to access and work on my website I would click the *Invite People* button and type in their email address and decide which roles I want them to have (figure 7.22). After I check all the roles I want this user to have I will then click the *Send Invite* button.

Then the person you invited would get an email similar to figure 7.23 and all they would have to do is click on the *Accept Now* button and they would be taken to the Wix website where they would click on the *Create Account & Accept* button as seen in figure7.24. Finally they would need to create a password for their new account, and they will then be logged in and taken to the Wix Dashboard for your website.

Settings > Roles & Permissions > Invite People to This Site

Invite People to This Site

Cancel   Send Invite

Give people access to this site and assign them roles. Learn more

Email(s) *

name@example.com

To add multiple invitees, enter each email separated by a comma.

Role(s) *

Select one or more roles for the people you're inviting. To create roles or edit permissions, go to Manage Roles.

General Roles

☐ Admin (Co-Owner)
Has full access to manage, edit & publish site, including billing, domains and inviting people, but cannot delete or transfer site. View Role Permissions

☐ Website Manager
Has access to manage, edit & publish site, but cannot manage billing, delete, duplicate or transfer site. View Role Permissions

☐ Website Designer
Can edit the site, manage settings and apps but cannot access Inbox, contacts and other sensitive info. View Role Permissions

☐ Back Office Manager
Can access the Dashboard to manage site settings and apps but cannot edit the site. View Role Permissions

Billing Roles

☐ Billing Manager
Can make purchases, manage subscriptions, add payment methods and connect a domain to the site. View Role Permissions

☐ Domain Manager
Can connect and manage domains but cannot make purchases. View Role Permissions

Blog Roles

Figure 7.22

Figure 7.23

Figure 7.24

When you go back to the Roles & Permissions section, you will then see this new user account listed with their associated role. If you need to edit their role then you can click on the ellipsis next to their name and choose *Change Role*.

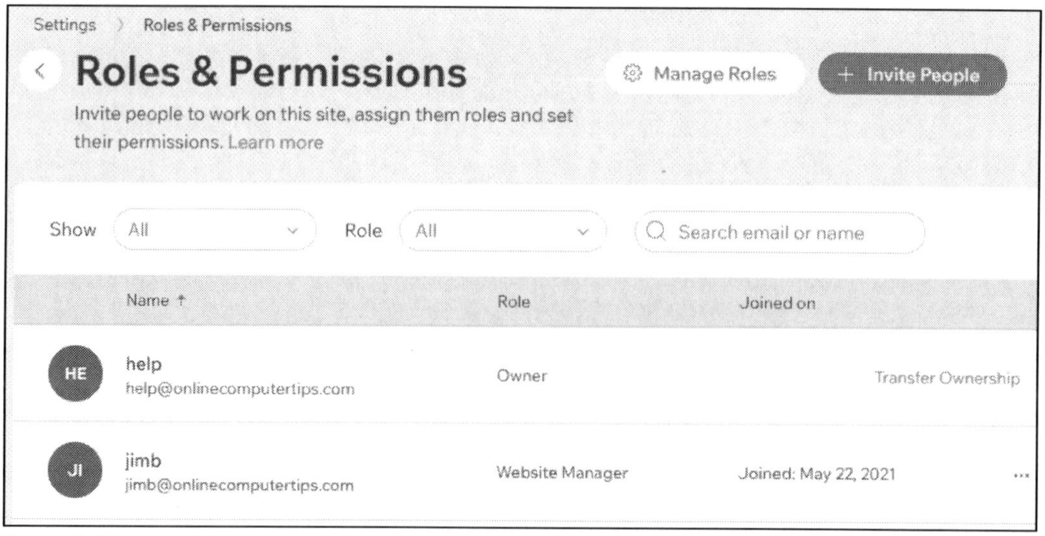

Figure 7.25

Transferring Site Ownership

If a situation arises such as you sell your business or even sell your website then Wix will allow you to transfer the ownership of your website to another person. This process is done from the same Roles & Permissions section we were just working in.

Once you are in Roles & Permissions, you will see a link that says *Transfer Ownership* next to your name. This is what you will need to click on to begin the process.

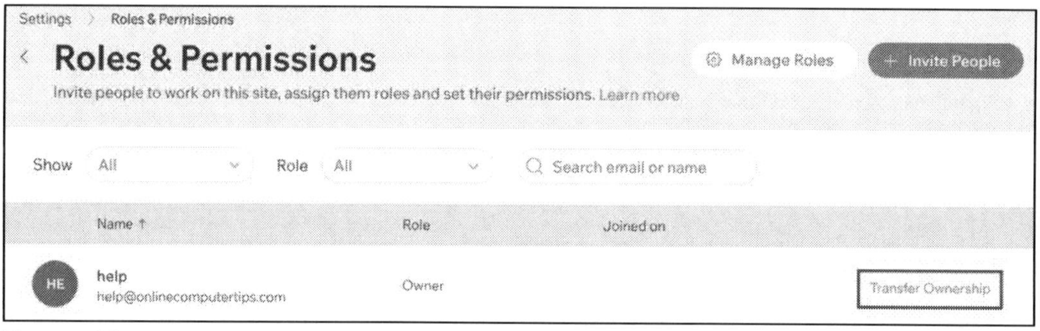

Figure 7.26

To transfer the ownership of your website to another person, you will need to enter their email address in the box where it says, "*Who will be the new site owner?*".

If you will still need access to the site to make changes then you can check the box that says *Keep my role as Website Manager of this site after the transfer*. If you want to save a copy of your website for your records or to use as a template for another site then you can check the box that says *Create a copy of this site and keep it in my account*.

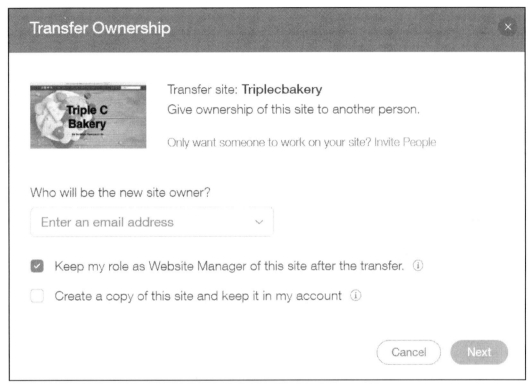

Figure 7.27

Once you fill in the email address and click the *Next* button you will be shown a confirmation screen and if everything looks correct, you can click on the *Transfer Ownership* button to complete the transfer.

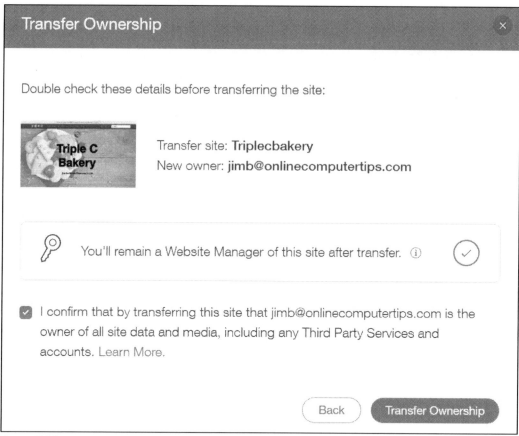

Figure 7.28

Restore Previous Versions (Site History)

When you are working on your website, you might come across a situation where you liked an older version or the way your site looked several changes ago. Rather than trying to undo all those changes or trying to make your site look the way it did before you made those changes, you can instead revert back to a previous version of your site using the Site History feature.

To access your website's history, you can click on the *Site* menu and then click on *Site History*.

Figure 7.29

When in the Site History section you have the option to view all of your previous revisions, only published revisions, versions you manually saved, or versions that you have marked as favorites by "starring" them.

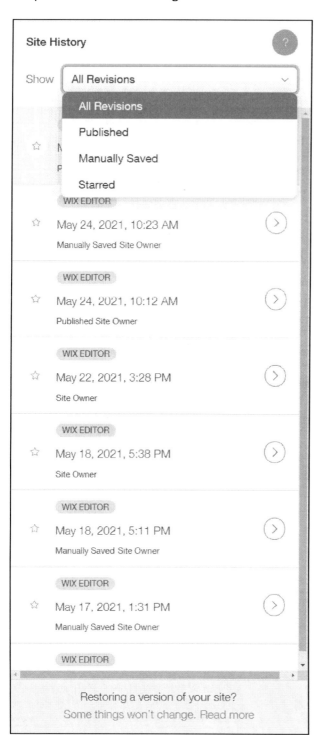

Figure 7.30

While reviewing your previous versions, you can click on the star icon to "star" them and also click on the pencil icon to rename a particular version so it's easier to find the next time you need to review it.

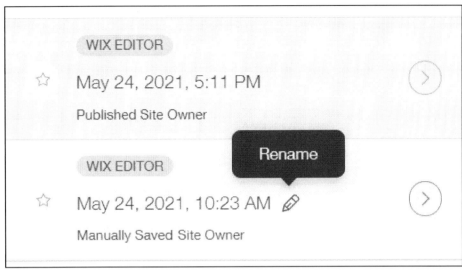

Figure 7.31

If you want to restore an older version and make it the current version then you can click on the arrow next to that version and then click on the *Restore* button.

Figure 7.32

 When you restore an older version of your website, customization and design changes will be reverted but there will be certain items that will not be affected such as blog posts, content of certain apps, your media gallery items, contacts and so on. Check the Wix website for a full listing.

Using the Search Bar to Find Wix Elements

I discussed adding a search bar to your website in the last chapter so your visitor could easily find content on your website. The Wix editor has its own search bar that you can use to find the features you need to use for your site editing tasks.

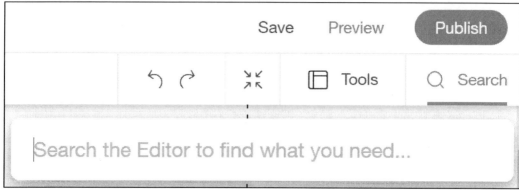

Figure 7.33

Let's say I wanted to add a PayPal button to my site so my visitors could make purchases and then pay for their items via PayPal. If I search for PayPal, I get several results and can then click on the one that looks like it would be what I am looking for (figure 7.34).

If I click on the result that says PayPal Button, I will then be taken to the Wix apps section where I can download the PayPal Button app and install it on my website (figure 7.35).

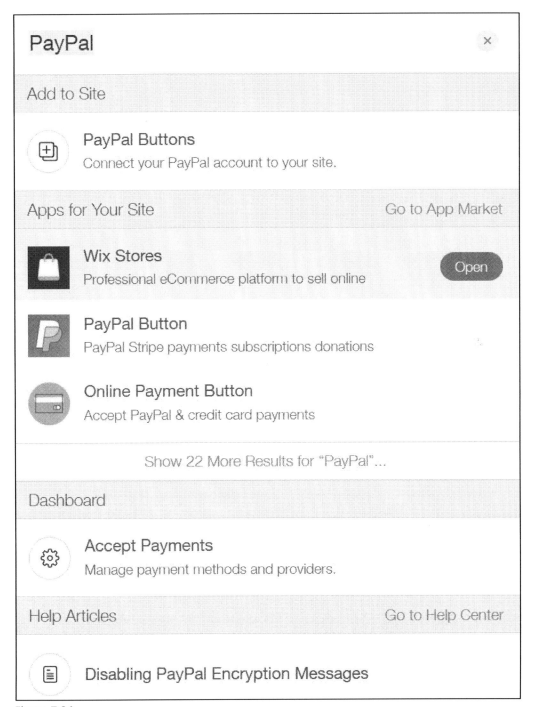

Figure 7.34

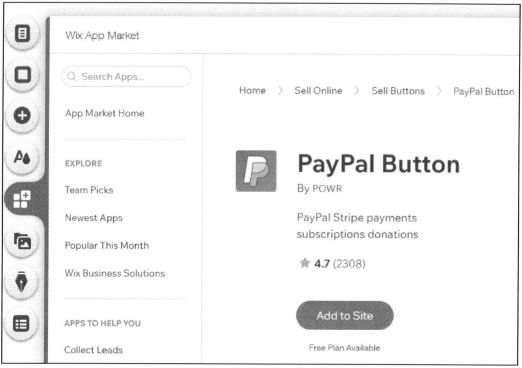

Figure 7.35

You can use this Wix search feature to find just about anything you need while creating your site so rather than spend your time searching menus or even Google, try the search bar feature instead.

Make a Duplicate Copy of Your Website
When creating a website you might encounter a situation where you would like to use the work you have done so far for a different website and still be able to continue on with your current site and not have to alter it for your new idea.

This is where making a copy of your website can come in handy. When you duplicate a site, Wix will take the current state of your website and then copy everything over to a new site. To start this process you will need to go to your *Wix Dashboard*, click on *Site Actions* and then choose *Duplicate Site*.

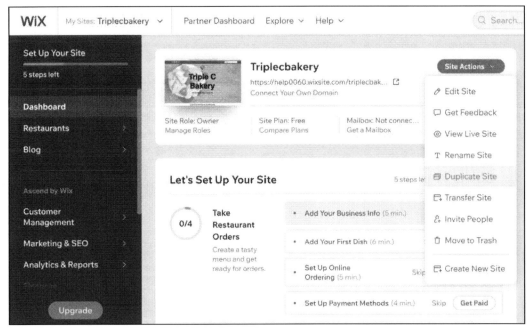

Figure 7.36

Now you will need to give your copied site a name or just stick with the name that Wix creates for you which is what I am going to do. Next I will click on the *Duplicate* button.

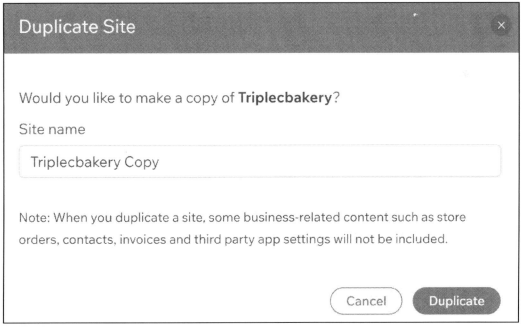

Figure 7.37

Now when I click on the *My Sites* dropdown in the Wix Dashboard, I will see my copied site that I can then click on to start editing. You can click on *Edit Site* from the Site Actions dropdown.

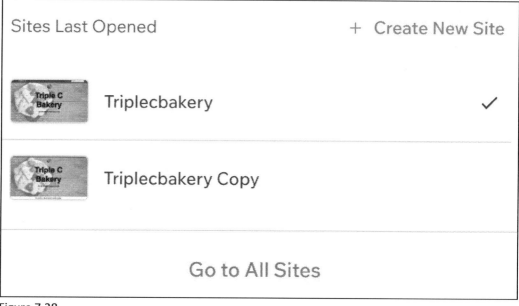

Figure 7.38

 There is no obvious way to see what website you happen to be working on in the Wix editor if have a copy of your site that looks exactly the same as the original. You might want to make a change that will make them stand apart from each other, so you don't end up editing the wrong one.

Mobile Editor\Viewer

Since everyone seems to work more from their smartphones than their personal computers, it makes sense that you would want your website to be "mobile friendly", meaning that you want it to look good and be easy to navigate on mobile devices.

When you click on the *Switch to Mobile* view in the editor, you might be presented with a *Meet Your Site on Mobile* wizard that you can go through to help you get started (figure 7.40).

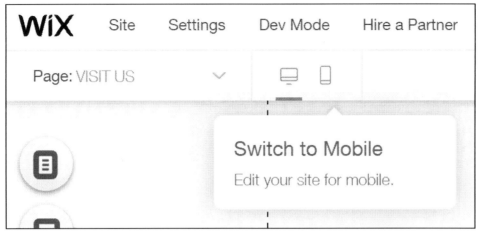

Figure 7.39

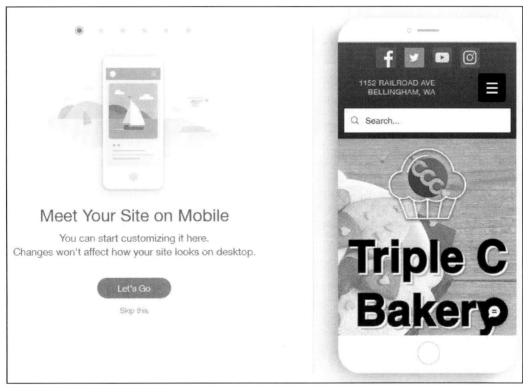

Figure 7.40

I will just skip the wizard and go right into edit mode. As you can see from figure 7.41, you get similar tools and options like you do for the desktop version, but things won't be exactly the same.

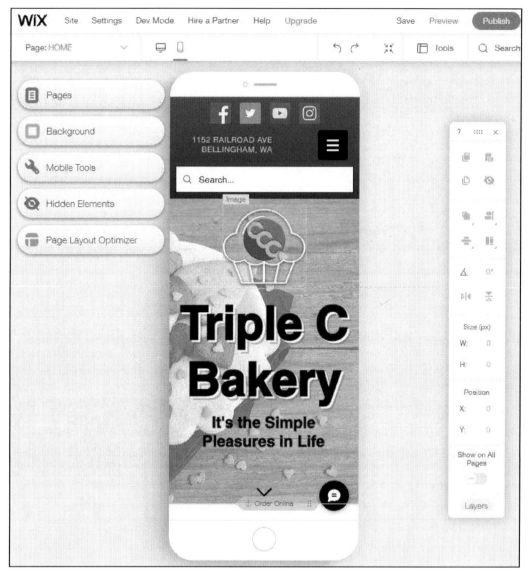

Figure 7.41

One thing you might want to do is run the *Page Layout Optimizer* to see if it makes your site layout look any better. I would first browse through your site on the mobile view and then run the optimizer and see how it looks after. If you don't like the changes it made you can always undo them.

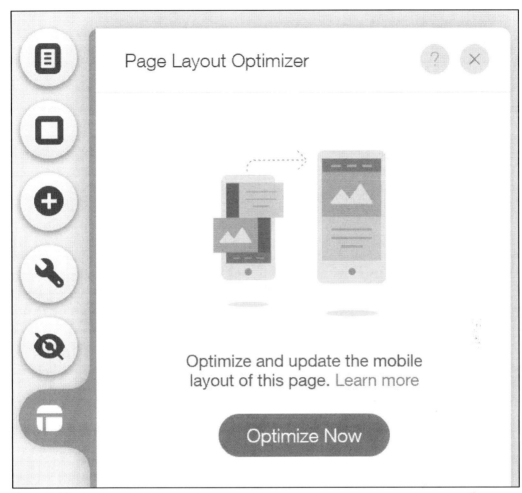

Figure 7.42

I would also check out the *Mobile Tools* to see if they can help optimize your site for mobile devices (figure 7.43). As you go through the tools and apply them to your site, the + signs will turn to green checkmarks.

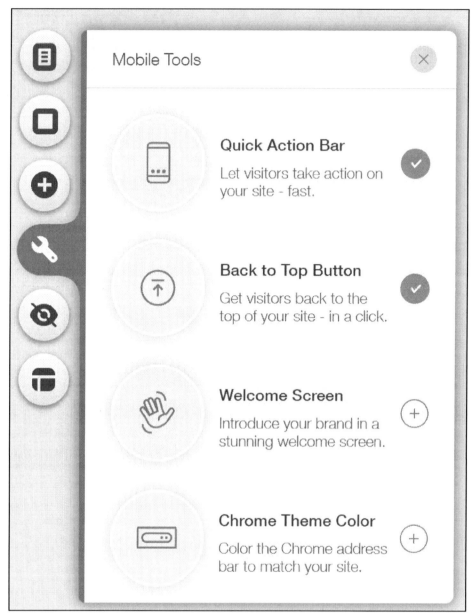

Figure 7.43

Here is what each selection will do.

- **Quick Action Bar** – This will add a button bar that will allow your visitors to do things such as call or email you, go to your Facebook page or chat with you with just the tap of a button. If you add this bar, you will need to configure each one of these items.

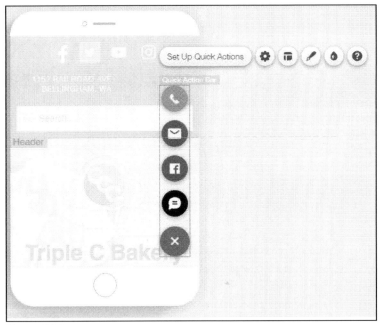

Figure 7.44

- **Back to Top Button** – Adding this feature will place a button on your page that your visitors can tap on at any time to bring them back to the top of the page.

Figure 7.45

- **Welcome Screen** – Here you can add a welcome screen with a custom logo and animation that your visitors will see when they first land on your site.

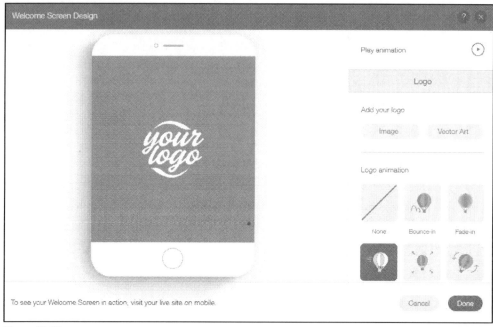

Figure 7.46

- **Chrome Theme Color** – Since Google Chrome is one of, if not the most popular web browsers in use today, you can add a custom theme color to your mobile site that will be displayed when viewed using Google Chrome.

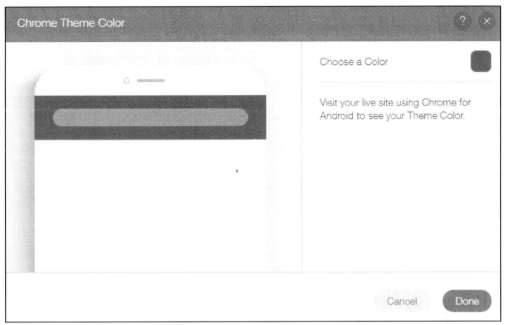

Figure 7.47

If you would like to learn more about Google Chrome and other popular Google apps such as Docs and Gmail then check out my book titled **Google Apps Made Easy**.
https://www.amazon.com/dp/1798114992

As you can see in figure 7.48, the *Add* button for the mobile version of the site doesn't have nearly as many choices as it does for the desktop mode. Then again, you are probably going to do most of your editing in the desktop mode and then switch over to the mobile mode and make any changes that might be required to have your layout look appropriate for mobile devices.

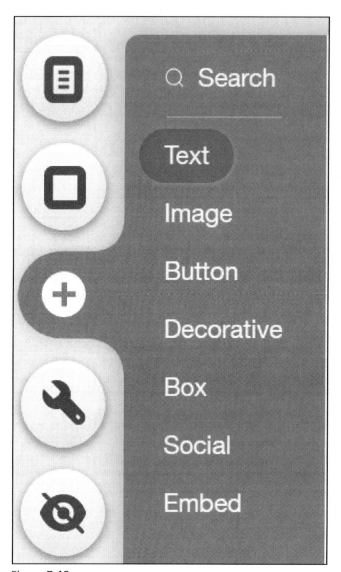

Figure 7.48

Chapter 8 - Publishing Your Website

The whole goal of creating a website is to eventually have it live on the internet so other people can see your products, services or ideas and hopefully share them with others and get you some sales… assuming you are selling something.

In order to have your website be live on the internet, you will need to publish your work, otherwise you will be the only one who will be able to see your website. Once your website is live, you will still be able to edit it and make changes whenever you need to so don't think it's a one-time situation and you have to have everything perfect before you go live.

Publishing and Unpublishing Your Website
The process of publishing your website (making it live) is a very easy process and it is also necessary to be able to view how certain changes will look on your site. I'm sure you have seen that Publish button at the top right corner of the screen staring at you while you were working on your site and were just dying to click on it. Well now is your chance!

Figure 8.1

Once you click the *Publish* button, you will be shown the URL for your website and also be offered an opportunity to search for and purchase your own domain name. You can then click on the *View Site* button to be taken to your live website. I would also copy that URL and paste it somewhere that you will be able to find it so it's easy to get to, so you don't need to come back to your Wix account to find your published website's address. You can also go to the Settings dropdown menu in the editor and choose View Published Site at any time to be taken to your live website.

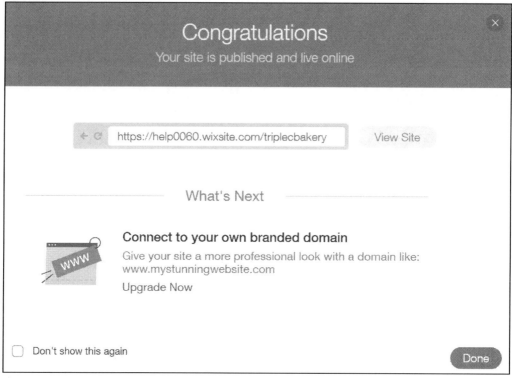

Figure 8.2

Once you are on your live website, you will want to go through all of your pages to make sure that everything looks correct, and nothing is getting cropped off the page or looks out of place. Just remember that different size screens and resolutions will affect how much of your page will be seen on the screen. This is why you should always keep your work within the gridlines.

If you ever need to unpublish your site for any reason in the future, it is a very easy process and only takes a couple of steps. First you will need to click on the Settings menu in the editor and choose *My Dashboard*. Once you are in your site dashboard you will click on *Settings* on the left side of the screen. Next, you will click on *Website Settings,* and you will see that it says your website is published with a link that says *Unpublish* that you can click on to have your site not be live any longer. Once you click on Unpublish, you will get a warning message telling you that nobody will be able to see your website any longer.

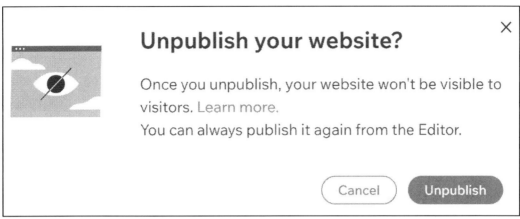

Unpublish your website?

Once you unpublish, your website won't be visible to visitors. Learn more.
You can always publish it again from the Editor.

Cancel   Unpublish

Figure 8.3

If you change your mind or want to publish your site again later, you can simply repeat the publishing process that I have previously discussed.

Change Your Website URL

When you created your website, Wix suggested a URL (address) for your site based on its name. If that name does not work for you or if you are going in a different direction with your website, then you can change it to something a little more fitting.

From the same website settings section where you saw the unpublish option, you will find the *Site address (URL)* section that will show your website's current address. Here you can change the last part of the address to something else if you like. The wixsite.com part of the address cannot be changed unless you connect your own domain to your Wix webpage.

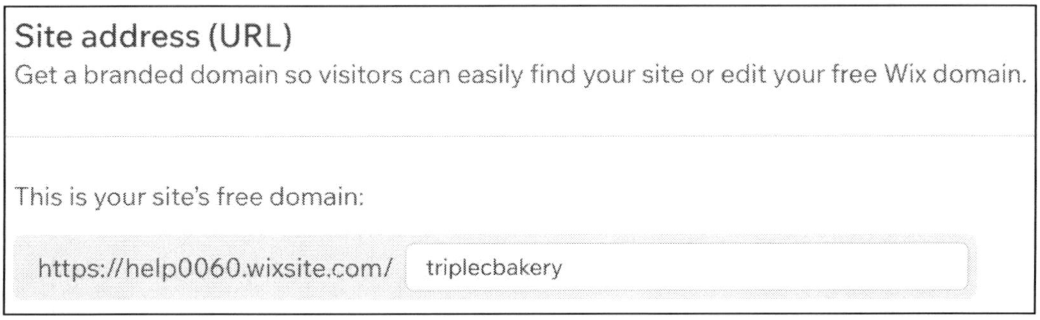

Site address (URL)
Get a branded domain so visitors can easily find your site or edit your free Wix domain.

This is your site's free domain:

https://help0060.wixsite.com/   triplecbakery

Figure 8.4

When planning the name of your website and its address, you want to make sure that you don't use an address that is too long and too hard to remember or type. If you do that then you will be missing out on potential visitors that can't remember your sites name or end up misspelling it and giving up.

Connect Your Domain or Get Your Own From Wix
If you are just creating a basic website for fun or for a hobby for example then you should be ok with the URL that Wix provides for you and just have them host your website for you for free. Unless you sign up for one of the premium plans to get more features that is.

If you already have a website domain name that you own then you can use that with your Wix site rather than the generic **wixsite.com** address that they provide but you will need to have a premium account to do this. If you don't have your own domain name then you can purchase one through Wix to make things a little easier when it comes to connecting your domain to your website.

If you go to the *Settings* menu and click on *Connect Domain* you will have an option to buy a new domain name or connect your existing domain.

Figure 8.5

If you choose the Buy a new domain name choice you can then search for the name you wish to use and find out if it's available or already taken.

Figure 8.6

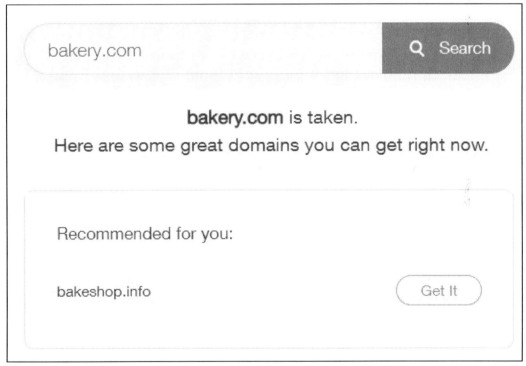

Figure 8.7

The steps for connecting a domain you already own requires a premium account before you can even begin the process. It will also involve some technical steps such as adding the Wix DNS (Domain Naming System) servers to the hosting account where you have your domain. Then you will need to wait a bit for the changes to take effect before you can verify the domain connection. I can't really show you this process since it varies depending on who you use for your site hosting and I don't want to really buy triplecbakery.com since I don't own a real bakery! You can use the Wix help to guide you through this process and it's really not too difficult. Plus your hosting company will most likely help you as well.

Wix Free SSL Certificate
With all of the online "cybercrime" going on, it's important to make sure that your website is secure and that your visitors feel safe when visiting your website and especially making purchases from your site.

One thing you should be doing when publishing a website is providing security via an SSL (Secure Sockets Layer) certificate. When this security layer is applied to your site, it ensures that the data and traffic between your computer and the website is encrypted and that nobody can read this information if they find a way to intercept it.

If you have ever paid attention to the address bar in your browser when you are on various websites, you might have noticed that the site address begins with https rather than http such as *https://onlinecomputertips.com/*. The **S** indicates that the site is secure and also has a security certificate applied. You might have also noticed the lock icon next to the website address indicating that the site is secure. Different browsers might have different looking icons for this feature.

Figure 8.8

If you don't have an SSL certificate installed on your website then you will not have a trusted site and you will also be penalized by Google for search indexing because it will consider your site not to be secure.

Fortunately when you use Wix for your website, they will provide you win a free SSL certificate and apply it to your site for you. They will also apply it to your website, so you don't need to worry about having a "professional" do it for you.

Getting a Custom Email Address
If you plan on using your new website for professional\business use then you might want to think of getting an email address for your account that matches your domain name. So rather than using something that doesn't look professional such as **triplecbakery@aol.com,** I can rather use an email address that looks something like **info@triplecbakery.com**.

To use a custom email address with your website, you will need to have one of the premium plans and then you can choose how many mailboxes (email addresses) you wish to have. Once you have your premium plan in place you can then go to the Settings menu and choose *Get a Mailbox.*

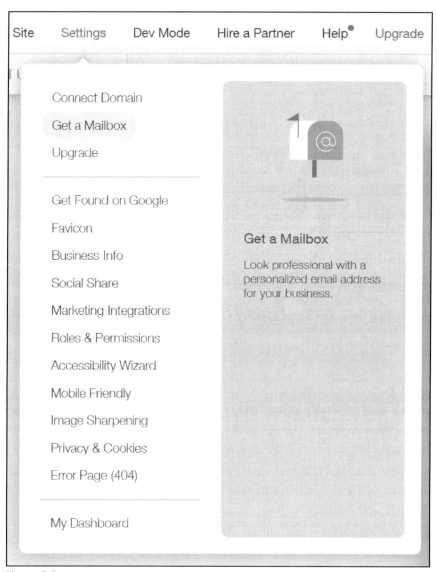

Figure 8.9

From there you would just choose your email name to go in front of **@yourdomain.com** and choose a password. If you already have an email address that you obtained outside of Wix then there will be some additional configuration required which will vary depending on where you go the email address from. You can then connect your Wix email address to your Gmail account if you want to use Gmail to read emails from your new email address.

What's Next?

Now that you have read through this book and learned how Wix works and how easily you can create professional looking websites, you might be wondering what you should do next. Well, that depends on where you want to go. Are you happy with what you have learned, or do you want to further your knowledge of web design with some more advanced website development software or even learn HTML coding?

If you do want to expand your knowledge and computers in general, then you can look for some more advanced books on web development or focus on a specific technology such as HTML, JavaScript or WordPress if that's the path you choose to follow. Focus on mastering the basics, and then apply what you have learned when going to more advanced material.

There are many great video resources as well, such as Pluralsight or CBT Nuggets, which offer online subscriptions to training videos of every type imaginable. YouTube is also a great source for instructional videos if you know what to search for.

If you are content in being a proficient Wix user that knows more than your coworkers and friends then just keep on practicing what you have learned. Don't be afraid to poke around with some of the settings and tools that you normally don't use and see if you can figure out what they do without having to research it since learning by doing is the most effective method to gain new skills.

Thanks for reading **Wix Made Easy**. If you liked this title, please leave a review. Reviews help authors build exposure. Plus, I love hearing from my readers! You can also check out the other books in the Made Easy series for additional, computer-related information and training.

And don't forget to stay up to date on my Made Easy Book Series website! **www.madeaseybookseries.com**

You should also check out my computer tips website, as well as follow it on Facebook to find more information on all kinds of computer topics.

www.onlinecomputertips.com
https://www.facebook.com/OnlineComputerTips/

About the Author

James Bernstein has been working with various companies in the IT field for over 20 years, managing technologies such as SAN and NAS storage, VMware, backups, Windows Servers, Active Directory, DNS, DHCP, Networking, Microsoft Office, Photoshop, Premiere, Exchange, and more.

He has obtained certifications from Microsoft, VMware, CompTIA, ShoreTel, and SNIA, and continues to strive to learn new technologies to further his knowledge on a variety of subjects.

He is also the founder of the website onlinecomputertips.com, which offers its readers valuable information on topics such as Windows, networking, hardware, software, and troubleshooting. James writes much of the content himself and adds new content on a regular basis. The site was started in 2005 and is still going strong today.

Printed in Great Britain
by Amazon

18814791R00124